# Learn First "Then Live Life"

### A Philosophy

You Should Begin Your Life
With The End In Mind

By:

## James A. Brown

Copyright ©2009 by James A. Brown. All rights reserved. Printed in the United States of America. No part of this book may be used or reproduced in any manner whatsoever without written permission, except in the case of brief quotations embodied in articles, reviews or educational material.

Cover Design by KDP

For information or permission contact author;
James A. Brown
Atlanta, GA 30321

## In Dedication To

**High School, Trade School, & College Students** who are in the foundational stages of making life decisions. May they seek wise counsel when deciding.

**Young Adults** everywhere who may still be searching for Direction & Purpose in life.

**Educators** whose task is to impart Knowledge & Understanding into all of us early on in life.

**Parents and Grandparents** who wish to give their children as much wisdom as possible before sending them on their life's journey.

**&**

**Everyone** who will seek to understand the biblical principle of "Sowing & Reaping"

# 8-Reasons To Read This Book
## It was written TO HELP:

1. Prevent Broken Dreams

2. Prevent Misdirection in life

3. Revitalize Hope in existing Lifestyles and/or Conditions

4. **Encourage Parents to talk to their Children & Grandchildren**

5. Overcome Mental and Physical Obstacles

6. Understand and Overcome Societal Distractions

7. Increase Confidence & Faith in Oneself

8. Create Productive & Fulfilled Citizens

# Table of Contents

| | | |
|---|---|---|
| Foreword | The Foreword | Page 6 |
| Chapter 1 | Career Choices | Page 8 |
| Chapter 2 | Road Signs – Road Blocks | Page 13 |
| Chapter 3 | Look Around You | Page 18 |
| Chapter 4 | Gifts, Callings, Purpose & Destiny | Page 21 |
| Chapter 5 | Peer Pressure | Page 25 |
| Chapter 6 | Lifestyles | Page 29 |
| Chapter 7 | Money Matters | Page 33 |
| Chapter 8 | Basic Living – Monthly Expenses | Page 38 |
| Chapter 9 | Having Credit & Making Debt | Page 42 |
| Chapter 10 | Seeking Employment | Page 50 |
| Chapter 11 | Emotional / Mental Preparation For Living Life | Page 56 |
| Chapter 12 | Relationships | Page 60 |
| Chapter 13 | Natural Frustrations | Page 64 |
| Chapter 14 | Have a Vision – Write Your Vision | Page 70 |
| Chapter 15 | It Doesn't Have To Be This Way | Page 75 |
| Chapter 16 | My Sowing & Reaping – Seedtime Harvest, Karma | Page 84 |

| | | |
|---|---|---|
| Chapter 17 | The Great Seed Planter | Page 88 |
| Chapter 18 | The Time Clock | Page 91 |
| Chapter 19 | Statistics To Consider | Page 93 |
| Chapter 20 | Suggested Career Choices | Page 96 |
| Chapter 21 | Questionnaire | Page 103 |
| Chapter 22 | If You Can | Page 106 |

# Foreword

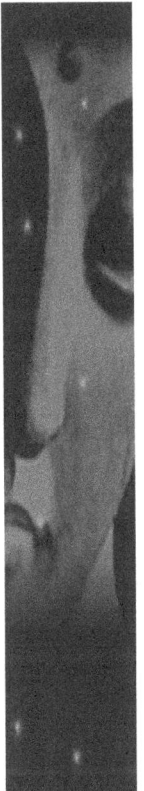

Many of us now look back on our lives and say; "**IF I ONLY KNEW BACK THEN WHAT I KNOW NOW**", my life would be different. I would have made better choices and decisions; I would have asked more questions; I would have taken a different route; I would have waited longer before I got married; I would have gone to college or taken up some kind of a trade; I would have joined the military; I would have started my career much earlier; I would have done more for my parents; I would have given my parents more honor and respect; I would have spent more time with my children; I would have finished college; I would have waited longer before I started a family; I would have taken better care of my body; I would have paid more attention to my dental health; I would have started saving and investing earlier, etc. The list goes on and on.

Having hindsight is everything. However, hindsight is too late when most of our life has passed us by and we can't go back and change things. We can only look back but we can't go back. So, what do we do with the information and the wisdom we have gained from our past? We should pass it on to the next generation so they can be much wiser when making those same decisions and choices that will affect them for the rest of their lives.

This book is the result of my learning some principles of life and wanting to share these principles with others. Those principles are ***Sowing & Reaping, Seedtime & Harvest, and the Law of Karma***. This simple guide will help any generation if they take time to read, listen, and learn. Nobody knows how long they will journey in this life. Nevertheless, if we could learn a few basic principles before starting off, we could make the journey with fewer headaches and disappointments in ourselves and in others. I have learned both by listening and not listening, reading and not reading. Hopefully, anyone who reads this book will take heed to these simple truths and apply them to their lives *before* their journey begins. Those who have already started can also gain insight and make appropriate adjustments. These are some of the insights that I have gained along my path.

From growing up on the farmlands of S.C., to earning a B.S. Degree in Electrical Engineering, a former U.S. Air Force Pilot, becoming a published Author, father of two children, my life's journey has encountered setbacks and disappointments along this path. Despite what appears to be a successful career, I had periods of uncertainties and made many mistakes in the process. Considering myself to be very intelligent and not needing a mentor or a life coach, I started my journey with only what I thought I knew about life. I inherit my father's boldness, his self-determination, and his life survival skills in my journey towards completing my dreams. But learning how to be a man, a husband, and a father while still growing up was not easy. Lifestyle changes, family dynamics, household management, relationships, money, credit cards, and world travelling came at a very fast pace. It became very challenging for me to face these realities of living the lifestyle that I was creating for myself. Although I made good career choices and decisions, I did not seek wise counsel when I should have…particularly in the areas of relationships and financial preparation for the later stages of my life. Those two areas have cost me plenty of time and money. **I didn't know that I didn't know.** Therefore, I had to learn from my many mistakes along the way. **Karma** came because of my good/bad choices and decisions. Only my determination to succeed kept me moving forward towards my dreams, purpose, and destiny. Now I say: *If I Only Understood Back Then what I Understand Now.* Having knowledge is one thing, but having a *real* Understanding of what you know *changes your life.*

Looking back, my whole life was based and is presently based on the **choices** I make. Therefore, karma implies the action of my conscious choice-making. And whether you like it or not, everything that is happening at this moment is a result of the choices you've made in the past. Unfortunately, a lot of us make choices unconsciously, and therefore we don't think they are choices--and yet, they are. You must become consciously aware that your future is generated by the choices you are making in every moment of your life

If you can receive the information contained in this book, it would be an investment for a lifetime...not only for yourself but also for those you love or care about. What price would you pay if you could adequately prepare yourself for your future? It has been said that "If you give a man a fish, you feed him for a day. But if you teach him how to fish, he can feed himself for a lifetime". This book will feed you wisdom and simple truths in all areas of your life.

The *spiritual* views and/or opinions expressed in the book are only a reflection of personal beliefs…although many people may share these same views and/or opinions. These views and/or opinions are not intended to change or redirect the spiritual beliefs of those who may read this book. However, the *natural* principles of "beginning and living" life expressed in this book are foundational truths. They are ill-respective of your spiritual belief system, national origin, gender, race, creed, or color. Please read with an open mind!

# Choices and Decisions…

# Chapter 1
# Career Choices

Having career choices and goals in life are great. The expression "Those who fail to plan, plan to fail" is so very true. However, there is also a practical side of life one must consider before venturing off into some great career plan. You can spend a lot of time planning for a career that won't financially support you or your family. It will just end up as being simply a "nice thing" to do or to know about. You may end up struggling trying to make a living in that career area. Consequently, you may have wasted a lot of time and effort on a career choice that will take you *nowhere*. Later you may regret choosing that area. This has been the case for many hopeful students and young adults when they have embarked upon life without: (1) no guidance or wisdom from elders, (2) no advice from those who are in that particular career field, and (3) no advice from those who may have been disappointed in that field. We all need to count the cost…short-term and long term before we begin. There are educational, emotional, and financial costs associated with any chosen career profession. Once we know the cost, we should ask ourselves are we willing to proceed.

We often choose careers because of the popularity, the excitement, or the glamour associated with that choice. We may even exhibit some of those same talents ourselves. We see people in those areas who appear to be successful. We sometimes never know the route they took to get to that point. We often choose that career field hoping that we would have the same measure of success as the ones we are watching. Oftentimes it's only a few out of thousands that get to that level of success. Moreover, if we don't personally reach *that* success status, disappointments often set in and we may resort to taking *other* jobs because we don't want to start all over again in another career choice. These other jobs sometimes do not come close to our original expectation. Consequently, the result of all this is that we *may* have; (1) wasted years of college or trade school, (2) accumulated debt with *limited* or *no* income source to service that debt, (3) placed a financial burden upon ourselves or parents to eliminate the debt, (4) be forced to live with our parents or relatives after college or trade school, and (5) possibly set up ourselves to have credit issues. If you default on student loans, financial institutions have many ways to obtained the money owed…to the extent of seizing income tax returns, and garnishing wages, etc. This financial and mental burden could last for many years.

We do ourselves a **"Great Disservice"** when we <u>limit</u> our career choices. A "good" plan without a "backup" plan can really hurt you in the long term.

Other people may see gifts in you that you can't see yourself. Therefore, we should choose our careers wisely with a secondary career as a backup from the beginning. We also must be open-minded to other career options as we proceed. You can increase your chances of success by taking additional subjects (if possible) while in your chosen course of study. This may enable you to go a different route if need be. However, you must stay abreast of industry trends. This will help you know what to expect down the road. While you're in school, talk to teachers, guidance counselors, other professionals, and industry personnel as you journey towards your intended destination. They are excellent sources of information about life and their career choices. Don't be afraid to ask any question. If you don't know what to ask, tell them that you don't know. If you find a person whose opinion you *highly respect*, ask them what they think of your career choice and what do they see in you. Ask them to be totally honest. This is the point where you must be open to hear what they will say. It may go against what you had already planned. The *worst thing* is for someone to agree with you on your career choice when he/she knows in their heart and experience that this may be a wrong choice for you.

If possible, seek more than one opinion. Be practical, sensible, and reasonable in your choice selection. For example: wanting to be a certain type of athlete (football player) when your physical size or skills may not support this type of sport. Having a plan "with options" will guide your steps.

***True Story:*** *I've always enjoyed sports. My favorite sports were basketball, baseball, and football. I was not a tall person (5'7") and not a big person (120 lbs.) in high school. I played baseball (a pitcher) in high school and in the local community. This was not much of a contact sport. I was pretty good in that sport. I also played basketball in elementary school but I was not a starter. Again, my size prevented me from fully engaging in that sport. Football was my least favorite because it involved* a lot of physical contact and there was a good chance of my getting seriously hurt because of my size. I could play all three sports in a limited capacity at that level. Nevertheless, I knew (genetically) that I would not grow much taller or become more physically developed whereas I could make a hobby or career out of playing sports. I was just being <u>real</u> with me. My natural parents were average sizes. The high price to pay to physically compete was not worth my sacrifice. (See Chart on Page 83)*

Being sensible, I decided not to pursue those hobbies and limited my involvement in high school sport activities. I concentrated on my main professional career desire. I decided to educate my mind and get the best grades possible...which I did. I became President of the Student Body and was involved in various honor clubs. I still kept the love of those sports in my heart and played them recreationally. Nevertheless, I knew that was as far as it would go. I was being practical and reasonable given my limited physical abilities. It was physically obvious to most people that my body was not meant for playing certain types of sports...especially for the sake of being popular. My friends often commented about my size. Their comments did affect me but I just pressed on.

Of course, I was somewhat disappointed that I couldn't play at a higher level in those sports. Most guys want admiration for something they could do physically and in other areas. I was no different. You might call this a "Guy Thing". This is probably still true today. Most guys will probably not admit this. Women may feel the same way in other areas when compared to each other and their personal views of life during their high school years.

**Exposing Your Dreams:** People will often make comments about what they think or feel about you. Sometimes it is best *not* to expose your dreams or plans to all of your friends. Remember, they are on the *same level* as you. Therefore, *no great advice or wisdom* can come from them. If they try to discourage you from pursuing your dreams, all that discouragement may become an obstacle in your mind. Seek authorities in those areas of interest.

But always remember; No matter *what* is said about you or *how* it is said, only *you* know how big your heart and desire is towards achieving your goals. Only you know your intimate thoughts and intensity towards your pursuit of your dreams.

***True Story:*** *My professional career desire was unusual during my high school era. (The 60s-70s). This desire came to me when I was about 10 years old. I was watching television and I saw what I wanted to do. Society would say that my desire was far from reaching and it would be a waste of time to pursue this dream. I knew this at the time because I researched and didn't find many "people of color" doing what I desired to do. Societal opposition was great as I perceived it. I kept this desire to myself all through my school years until the last month of my senior year. I even kept this hidden from my best friends. I only told my mother about my secret dream. My teacher asked the class about our dreams and goals. I started not to tell my classmates my true desire but I did. When I did, the whole class laughed at my desire. They said that people* *in my race didn't do these kinds of things. They said I was too short and too skinny for what I wanted to do. Of course, those comments affected me but it did not deter me. I said to myself; "they don't know how big my heart is towards this". This incident taught me a lesson and made me realize that if I had exposed my true dream to my friends and classmates early on, I probably would have heard these comments for a long time and it could have affected me whereas I may have changed my mind...but I didn't. When I entered college, I found other people who were interested in pursuing that same profession as I was. It then became very easy to share my thoughts, goals, and dreams with them.*

**The College Life**: College life can be exciting and scary at the same time. You are finally away from your home environment and have the freedom to do as you please with no one but you to watch over you. This is where your own motivation must begin to keep you focused on what you plan to do after your time in college is up...whether it be a two- or four-year stay. College life is also filled with distractions of the social and gender order. Some students never complete college because of these distractions. Your freedom to go and do as you please can get you into a lot of emotional situations and circumstances that getting good grades becomes a *secondary* issue. Without a proper foundation, personal determination, and your dreams/plans/goals, you can easily be swayed from what really matters and why you entered college in the first place. I have personally witnessed students who became career students. They never graduate. They become entangled in the college lifestyle and are trapped. They are afraid to venture out into the real world of individual responsibilities so they hold onto this temporary freedom. Reality finally steps in and they realize that they don't fit in any more. They slowly fade away without obtaining that degree or the degree has become forever in obtaining. Don't let this happen to you. Don't be ensnared by the college lifestyle. Stay focused and informed concerning your intended career choice.

In these changing times with *uncertain* futures, it's imperative that you don't get complacent while in college. You need to "think smart and be wise" concerning your future. Continue to look for better ways to improve your mind. "A mind is a terrible thing to waste". It has also been said that "Necessity is the Mother of Invention". But I say to you, never let *necessity* force you to use your inventive skills. Use them at all times. New inventions are happening at all times.

While in college, don't be consumed by today's fads and the sometimes "carefree" lifestyles. There is a price to pay for everything you do. The expression; "pay now and play later" or "play now and pay later" is very true. You should **pay now** by getting the best out of your college education. Make that sacrifice.

***True Story:*** *An engineering classmate of mine became very excited and eager to pledge a fraternity during our sophomore year in college. Our engineering advisor advised him not to pledge during this time because his grades were just average and they could suffer. Our advisor was very concerned about our timing when any one of us was considering engaging in activities outside of engineering. He knew our chosen course of study imposed great demands on our study time. My classmate <u>opted not</u> to accept that advice and decided to pledge. He successfully pledged but his grade point average for that semester was a 0.6. Our engineering class was made aware of this when our grades were posted. This was a good example of not making wise choices and decisions. My classmate's ensuing fraternity lifestyle eventually made him withdrawn from engineering and from college. There was nothing wrong in becoming a "frat" member because I became one during my senior year. I just made the right choice at the right time based on my grades and the time I could afford to sacrifice towards becoming a member.*

# Be Sure You Get To This Point & The Celebration!

# Don't Become A Career Student!

## Chapter 2
## Road Signs-Road Blocks

In our everyday travels from point A to B to C, etc., we encounter some of the signals and signs in the above illustration. If we don't take heed, we risk having accidents, getting lost in the process, getting frustrated, giving up and not reaching our destination. From your starting point (high school, college, or trade school) to your final destiny (career profession) is not always a straight path. No matter what plan or road you may have mapped for yourself, things could change. You must be open to changes and directions.

It would be great to see all "Green Lights" as you travel but oftentimes that is not reality. You may see; caution lights, detour signs, warning signs, yield signs, dead end signs, and stop signs. If you encounter a stop sign, TAKE HEED! It would be best to make a decision at that point rather than to press blindly ahead...not knowing what to expect. The best course of action to take in any given trip is to carefully preplan...meaning to anticipate possible changes.

**Self-Imposed Road Blocks**: You can create your own personal road blocks by being stubborn, hardheaded, and disrespectful, etc. These behaviors are self-imposed road blocks for any direction you may choose. However, these can be removed by simply changing your attitude. But there are other road blocks given by life that are not so easily removed. To overcome an inborn physical and/or mental disability can be very difficult. But many have managed to overcome these road blocks despite the odds for their intended direction and purpose in life. Life does not always deal a *"fair hand"* to play its own game. Plus, the game rules of life can change at any given moment or at any age. Things just happen.

**Check Ahead:** It can be highly upsetting when you thoroughly prepare for a career profession and later find out that the career field is declining or has limited jobs. Remember, road signs or road blocks are only *relevant to your intended direction* and purpose for your life. What could be a "Stop Sign" for you could be seen only as a "Caution Light" for someone else. Therefore, when making long trips (2-4 years of college/trade school), it is best to regularly check ahead to see if what you're seeking is still a viable plan. We need to check ahead at "critical points and times" in our educational journey. At the end of each year in school, check with teachers and career professionals. You should obtain industry projections and information concerning your career choice. Get help in analyzing the results. If the results are favorable, then press on. If not, rethink and re-plan. Ask for assistance if you must re-plan. You may reach your destination eventually, but it may require your taking a different route to get there. You may incur a delay (a secondary career choice) in the process. So be very observant as you travel emotionally and mentally towards your destination or career.

***True Story:*** *I wanted to become a USAF Pilot with a chance to see the world. I searched for a University that offered AFROTC. However, I also had to choose a course of study. My grades were good in all my high school studies so I could have chosen almost any field. I started to choose Journalism because I enjoyed writing. However, when I researched and saw that my chances were slim to none in terms of being a very successful journalist, I changed my mind. So, I said if I am unable to become a Pilot for any reasons, what major can I choose that will assure me a job when my flying career is done or if I am unable to get into flying? I chose engineering because I knew that field would always have job options. There are also other career areas with guaranteed job options. My good grades also helped me get a student loan during my freshman year. But my sustained good grades, along with my determined desire to become a Pilot, enabled me to receive a 3-year AFROTC scholarship for my remaining years. I did become an Air Force Pilot for 11 years and I have worked as an Electrical Engineer for the Federal Government. But guess what? I still write (books, poems, papers) as a hobby. Moreover, I have done this since high school…many years later. If my original desire was to become an Engineer, I could have chosen Engineering with AFROTC as a backup plan. A Military Officer option after college is a great backup plan for any graduate. I chose the Air Force. There are great career professions in the all the Armed Services.*

Having a desire for a "particular" profession that will not financially support you doesn't make you a failure nor does it invalidate your career choice. Not at all! All it means is that "at the present time" your career choice may not provide a promising future. But you don't have to give up your desire. The *Common-Sense* thing to do is to find a way to gain knowledge of that "desire" and make it a "hobby". Then you won't lose your interest in that field. Having done that, you should now begin college or trade school with the intent of acquiring a skill, a certificate, or a degree in what you know will support yourself, your intended lifestyle, and your family. Later on, in life, that "interest or hobby" may afford you the lifestyle you originally desired.

*True Story:* *A college classmate of mine chose Art Design as a major during the 70's. She chose this field because she had a gift of drawing and wanted to develop this gift much further. Her parents encouraged her to pursuit this as a career. She had great skills and made good grades in High School and College. She also was involved in the marching band. I met her during my sophomore year. She really enjoyed what she was doing and was looking forward to having a career in Art Design. However, she did not check ahead to see industry trends. Nor did she checked with industry professionals, or regularly confer with teachers, etc., about her intended destination. She just pressed on. Her parents didn't bother to check either. Everyone assumed that it should not be a problem for her to start a career after graduation.*

*After graduation, she found out that the jobs in her chosen career field were very limited because the industry had changed to using computers as a tool for Art Design majors. Computers were not part of her Art curriculum at that time. She did not want to return to college to start an additional study of computers as it related to Art Design. Therefore, she ended up not finding a job in that career field. She later told me if she had known earlier, she could have majored in Art Education (Teaching) instead of Art Design. Alternatively, she could have transferred to a different college with computer applications for Art Design before she graduated. Since then she has had many different jobs (retail stores, childcare jobs, substitute teaching, etc.). She did manage to integrate some of her artistic skills within the school system on a limited basis. However, these jobs have never been fulfilling to her inner-self. She still loves to draw (freestyle) but she has never worked in that career field. She has also managed to accomplish personal noteworthy projects outside of that career field and has been recognized by many for her great skills. But what she didn't know initially during her educational process did cost her 4 years of college education. Moreover, it gave her more than 25 years of frustrations and disappointments in the years that followed. Fortunately, when she married, her spouse's career choice was enough to help her maintain a good standard of living.*

Art Design was not a bad choice at the time and she could have possibly made a good living in that field. However, the Art Industry was changing to a new form of computerized art and she didn't know to prepare herself for that change. She was totally involved in her course of study. Although she had parents and teachers, she was *ultimately responsible* for herself as it related to her career. Unfortunately, some parents don't check or don't know how to check ahead for their children; nor, is it the teacher's responsibility. Teachers can also be fully engaged in *teaching* whereas they may not check ahead for industry trends. Textbooks are generally updated every 3-5 years so the information contained may not be totally reliable. In today's world, a lot could change in 3-5 years.

**True Story:** *My niece made excellent grades in high school mathematics but she also enjoyed writing. She asked my opinion concerning choosing a career profession. At the time, I was well into my professional occupation as a Pilot. I advised her to pursue a career involving math because I knew this field would always have job opportunities. She did not take my advice. Instead she chose to major in Journalism at a "very reputable" university. Upon graduation in 1985, she could not successfully start a career in that field. It had limited jobs and was highly competitive. She later told me that she regretted not taking my advice. She also has had many different jobs since then.*

Being a successful journalist is not an impossible task. There are many who have achieved this status. My nephew is a part time successful journalist. But his primary job is a Banker. The question is what does being "successful" mean to you as it relates to journalism or to any chosen profession. Can you emotionally, mentally, and financially survive in this field or any career choice?

Now my former classmate and my niece look back but can't go back. To start over much later in life is sometimes difficult, though not impossible. A more "determined" mind-set may be needed for this. By not checking the road signs of life and adhering to them, you can literally *drive* yourself to a disappointing future.

**Having Foresight:** I knew what I wanted to do in life early on. Therefore, I was very careful to preplan my career choice and direction. Fortunately, I chose wisely *before* I started my life's journey. In addition, I had a backup plan that would *guarantee* me other career options once my primary choice had ended. I could pilot the aircrafts shown below.

I was determined to succeed in accomplishing my dreams and goals. I mentally overcame my physical size as far as flying an airplane. We all can be taught if we are willing to listen and learn. I also gave myself the opportunity for success by: (a) studying hard, (b) doing what I needed to do, (c) keeping myself in line with my habits and activities, (d) knowing when and who to avoid, (e) knowing what was required of me for this occupation, (f) checking ahead, and (g) believing in myself. If a person can be reasonable, practical, and sensible about career choices, following this example can apply to *any* career profession they might choose.

Of course, there were many sacrifices made in achieving one of my goals and dreams. There were difficult times I had to face. I had to endure some pressing moments which were mentally, emotionally, and physically exhausting. Nevertheless, I counted the cost *before* I started and was prepared to pay the cost. During this experience, I kept looking ahead to the outcome of my training. The pinning on and the wearing of the U.S. Air Force Pilot Wings was worth the perseverance. I also had the support and prayers from my family and friends. But the *bottom line* was how much I really wanted this dream.

The only thing or person that could stop me from completing this dream was *me*. The opportunity was in front of me and all the provisions were placed at my disposal. There was no guarantee that I would complete pilot training. But I knew if I stayed focused, I had a great chance of completing training and wearing my Pilot Wings. I kept all unnecessary distractions out of my life. I wasn't about to let "me stop me" from finishing this task. I remained focused. I was fully aware of all requirements necessary to accomplish this dream of mine. How focused are you in your pursuit of your goals and/or dreams?

Captain James A. Brown
USAF Pilot

## Chapter 3
## Look Around You

**E**veryone you see started from "a beginning". The question is where have they ended up or where will they end up? Sometimes you can observe their habits/character and predict where they will end up...their destiny. Some will progress and some will stay stagnant. Look at the adults in your life and see what positions they are in. Are these positions admirable? Do you want to be like them in their current state of existence? If not, ask yourself what you need to do to *avoid* that state or lifestyle. Better yet, ask them if they would share with you about their life. Chances are that they started with "good intentions" and with great thoughts. They would more than likely tell you some of the mistakes they made. I believe you will find three common denominators in all situations; (1) I planned without seeking wise counsel. Or, I did plan by seeking wise counsel, (2) I didn't consider other options. Or, I did consider other options, and (3) I didn't look far enough down the road. Or, I had help looking far down the road. You should really listen and see how this advice can help you. You can't put a price on wisdom and understanding. Life is about choices. Your wise choices require getting wise counsel.

*"Sow a <u>thought</u> reap a habit; sow a <u>habit</u> reap a character; sow a <u>character</u> reap a destiny".* <sub>Stephen Covey</sub>

**Getting Good Counsel:** Your family members and friends may care about you; but it's about you and *your future*. It's your *choices* and *decisions* that will determine where you end up in life. It is how you receive good advice and how you apply that advice that makes the difference. Being determined and focused will guarantee you a high probability of success. Even this will be tested as you proceed along your course. Stay in touch with those who you are sincerely listening to. Keep asking questions concerning your chosen path. Only consult with those who have had the experience of living life. And particularly, consult with those who are in the profession that you desire to be in. Listen to all the pros and cons to make an informative choice and decision.

This is the time to thoroughly research "chosen" professions to see the potential for your success or failure and decide whether to embark or not. If your chosen profession does not look promising, consider another direction. Or, if you have already started and decided that you <u>do not</u> want to give up that "interest", you have a few options:

| | |
|---|---|
| 1. | Find another profession that you are also capable of doing that will afford you a career and the ability to support yourself and your family. This may prolong your stay in college or trade school. |
| 2. | Make your first "chosen" profession a "hobby" instead of a profession. |
| 3. | If you are in college, see if there is a possibility of changing majors and using some credit towards that new major. Consider having a "minor" in an area where you know you can find employment. |

**Open Your Eyes:** Being fully engaged in a "course of study" and not looking ahead or around you is not wise. It's like swimming in the "ocean of life" with your head in the water and not looking to see if you are going in the right direction. You must come up for air and look to see if the finish line is still reachable. If you just come up for air and <u>don't</u> open your eyes, the finish line could have disappeared. If it has, you should stop, tread water, and figure out what you must do or choose another direction. You could become a target for the "sharks of life" such as defeatism, doubt, weariness, anxiety, fear, etc. They may eventually attack you. Or else you may decide to give up and drown in your frustrations and disappointments.

You must also be aware that things do have a way of changing and the best laid plans sometimes go to naught. *The only thing constant is change itself.* You deceive yourself when you don't understand this principle. It is impossible to predict and prepare for every event or circumstance. But you can have elements or people in place to help you when things do change.

Being **stubborn** to receiving advice concerning the issues of life can and will cost you. Trying to *go your own way*, be your *"Own Man"* or be your *"Own Woman"* only plays to the winds of life that can toss you to and fro. We make a grave error in judgment when we think we are fully grown and/or matured just coming out of high school or finishing college. We need people in our lives who are *solidly grounded* and who we can lean on for advice as we travel through life. This does not mean that you can't make decisions by yourself; not at all. All it means is that you have exercised wisdom and good judgment by seeking wise counsel before deciding on a course of action.

**True Story**: *When I began my career as a College Graduate, an Air Force Officer, and a Pilot, it seemed like the financial agencies knew it too. They began to flood me with credit offers (store cards, bank cards, etc.). All of them were "instant" approval by my signature alone. I was somewhat <u>advised</u> not to accept these offers, but I did. I obtained 10 credit cards over a ten-year period…not thinking that my career may come to an end one day. I was living <u>high</u> in the moment. Well my flying career did come to an end but my credit card debt and bills didn't. During my transition period between careers, all my bills became late and my <u>great</u> Credit Score took a nose dive. I was left to do the best I could with my debts and my bills. I should have been thinking ahead, planning, and seeking advice from those who had travelled my same path. By not doing this, it cost me dearly in a lot of areas of my life.*

*I was totally engaged in living my life that I did not stop to look ahead to see the possible realities. Financial issues can affect more than just you. Since having adequate finances relate to our quality of life, anything or anyone who is a part of our quality of life will be affected also. It's a ripple effect that goes in all directions and affects all areas of your life.*

We all have said at times, "I should have listened back then when that advice was given to me". This is nothing unusual. It has happened and will happen to everyone. But when the "not listening or not heeding" the advice causes you uncomfortable situations, then it really hits home. In some cases, it's hard to recover from these kinds of decisions.

Without having someone to advise you as you continue your course in life, costly mistakes could be made. If it's only you "watching over yourself", you reduce the chances of achieving your dreams. It's a conscious decision that can cost you dearly. Your dreams could all but disappear in your sea of hopelessness. **Why take that chance?**

Life Coach!!

# Chapter 4
# Gifts, Callings Purpose & Destiny

There are "innate gifts" in all of us. Some may say that these gifts are given by God. But all of us will acquire many other talents/skills as we go through life. It's a process of growing up. We learn to do a lot of things that we didn't know years before. However, some things are just natural for us to do. I have the gift of writing. This gift has evolved over a period of years. This book is an example of that gift. It would be great if we could make a good living doing what we like to do. In many cases, that is very possible. Even doing so will still require some additional education and training.

Direction and guidance can come in many ways. Those who are "spiritually guided" will eventually find their purpose and destiny. Therefore, it would not matter what society says in terms of "what is the best career to go into". If you are destined to be an engineer, teacher, nurse, dancer, musician, writer, computer operator, sanitation engineer, store worker, mailman, housewife, gardener, etc., then it wouldn't matter what society says. You will become what you are destined to be. You will be happy and content. But even without any religious understanding or convictions concerning God, this principle still applies. Each of us has a purpose in life as to why we were born. There is a place and/or position in life when we know that "this is it". Most of us already feel this inside. We only must get to that place and/or position.

Nevertheless, in the absence of God in our decision-making process, we still need sound natural advice in the direction we choose to take. We need this advice early on so we don't waste years trying to figure things out and end up regretting that we didn't listen sooner or see other options. Preferably, this advice should come in high school or sooner before we get to college or trade school. College or trade school should be an exciting 2-4-year adventure for a "**true**" head start towards your intended future/destiny. So why have a 2-4 year "**false**" start only to find out you must start all over again on a different course.

I heard a quote by a college professor which says; *learn* something in your 20's; *become* something in your 30's; and *have* something in your 40's. But even better than that; you can learn, become, and have something much earlier in life if you seek wisdom and get wise counsel. You don't need to struggle for 20-30 years in order to have something. If your life is guided by clichés and old fables, then whatever you attached your hopes to is what you will become. I heard another man say, *"Whoever has your ear has your destiny in their mouth"*. Listen to the right kind of people.

**True Story:** *A good friend of mine wanted to pursue an Acting career because she saw images of that on television and it was very appealing. She really felt that she could make a career being an actress. This was something admirable and she saw herself being a star one day. With no outside guidance or wise counsel, she would have actively pursued that profession. However, her mother saw other innate gifts and talents in her. While she was very young, her mother noticed her coming to the aid of relatives and friends when they were in pain or got injured. This was something that she did instinctively. Her mother saw her as being employed in the medical profession one day. Therefore, her mother encouraged her to pursue a nursing career. In fact, she insisted that she go into this field. My wife took her advice and pursued this profession. She became a LPN and has been doing this for over 35 years. She never regretted listening to her mother in pursuing her God given gifts and talents. She really enjoys doing what she is doing. She later had to use those same talents in the medical care of her own mother.*

Some gifts and talents are obvious. Others may not be known or take time to develop. Most of us don't know what we are capable of doing or what our "calling" might be. It may take someone else to show us and tell us about ourselves. I was told that I have a trusting attitude towards people. As children or as young adults we should be ready to listen. So often, that is not the case. Your innate gifts and acquired talents will support your "Calling" and may lead to your purpose and destiny in life. Learn how to recognize them or ask help from others. If you don't, you will become subject to your own counsel and may proceed on paths that may never be fulfilling to your inner self. Develop your gifts and talents and choose a career that's best for you
*(See Potential Career Choices page 84)*

**Job Stops:** There will more than likely be some temporary "job stops" in route to where you would like to be. Part time jobs while in high school or college, community jobs, and retail jobs, are part of our learning and searching during our adolescent and young adult years. Most of these jobs are service oriented and we become part of that service industry. These jobs are vital in our development as productive citizens. Sometimes we make decisions early on to pursue careers in this industry.

Career jobs in the service industries will always be around. Any job that provides a service to the community will have opportunities for employment and should provide a reasonable standard of living and quality of life. Entrepreneurship is very prevalent in this industry. You can exist with minimal skill levels or high skill levels. One of the online definitions for the Service Industry is;

> *From cutting the grass to providing health care to delivering packages, service industries in the United States play an integral part in the daily activities of millions of people and businesses. These services may offer an improved standard of living, professional and technical expertise, or other essential services. The providers of such services involve all sectors of the economy including for-profit private businesses, non-profit organizations and various levels of government.* Business Encyclopedia

**True Story**: *A coworker shared a story with me. When he was 12 years old his uncle dropped by while he was playing with his friends. His uncle then called him out from the group. He reluctantly came over and was asked a question; "How much money do you have in your pocket?" He said he didn't have any. Right away his uncle asked him to come with him in his truck. He didn't want to go and he wasn't sure where they were headed. They arrived at a hardware store and walked in. His uncle instructed him to pick out the best lawn mower he wanted. Naturally he picked out the best according to his taste. His uncle then told him to pick out the best rake...which he did. His uncle paid for both. He was totally awed with what had just happen. His uncle told him that he could repay him by going back to his neighborhood and start cutting grass. He did just that and became self-sufficient in securing his own money. He said that day changed his life forever. He now thanks his uncle for giving him a life changing skill early on and had stirred an entrepreneurial spirit in him. He is now doing the same thing with his son.*

How you choose to enter this industry and how you choose to develop your skills is entirely up to you. All of us are unique in our own special way and there are jobs that seem to be "tailor-made" for us. We all must start somewhere in our quest to find our niche. In securing some types of jobs, we will discover where we don't want to be. But sometimes it may take an "uncomfortable" job or an uncomfortable "situation" to point us in the right direction. But where ever you find yourself and there are decisions to be made, get help in analyzing and deciding if this is where you fit in.

Swallowing your pride or not "ego tripping" could prevent you from taking certain paths that are bound to cause you problems in the long term. Always listen to the kind of people who want the best for you and who *know* how to advise you. Make sure that you should know who they are. There may be many voices trying to direct your path.

The below signs shows you some of the many people and entities who will try and direct your life. There is no right or wrong in any of the ones shown below. It all depends on what you want to do and the direction you want to take. If you want to be a teacher, then talk to teachers who are still teaching and those who have retired in that career field. Ask them as many questions as possible so you will know for yourself what all that profession would entail. Also, go online.

***True Story:*** *When I was in AFROTC in college, one of my instructors was a former Air Force Pilot. I spent many hours with him discussing his background, his desires, and what he did to earn his Pilot Wings. His advice was priceless and it really helped me when I entered Pilot Training. He had my undivided attention.*

**"Whoever Has Your Ear, Has <u>Your Destiny</u> In Their Mouth"**

Who or What Are You Listening To?

## Chapter 5
# Peer Pressure
*Self-Identity*

What is peer pressure? Where does it come from? How intense is it and how do you deal with it? When we hear the expression "Peer Pressure" we immediately associate this term to something not good. The word "Peer" is defined as: "A person who is equal to another in abilities, qualifications, age, background, and social status". The word *pressure* suggests or implies using force to move something or someone in a certain direction. (*Def: to force someone toward a particular end; influence*) But it doesn't say how much pressure, the frequency of the pressure, or how long the pressure is applied. Combining the two terms we get this online definition of Peer Pressure:

*"Social pressure by members of one's peer group to take a certain action, adopts certain values, or otherwise conforms in order to be accepted".*

This is about our "conforming to be accepted" by persons and/or groups. Who are these persons and who are these groups? What kinds of people and what types of groups are we talking about? There is a wide range of possibilities in both areas. There are positive peer pressures and there are negative peer pressures. Positive peer pressure can be defined as the type that has a positive effect on your character, thus affecting your life. It is beneficial and helpful to your overall well-being and state of mind. Negative pressure has the opposite effect. There are countless articles, videos, books, and papers on peer pressure. They give examples of types of peer pressure and how to deal with it. Rather than follow in that same vein of thought, let's talk about why is peer pressure so effective. Why do people succumb to this pressure? I believe it all comes down to **Self-Identification**. Do you know who you are inside? Who has defined you? Have you defined yourself? Who are you aligning yourself with to form a personal identity? Have you discovered a part of you that thinks for itself and it does not always agree with what is being said or done around you? When we are young, our initial identity is often defined by someone else. Hopefully it's our parents. If not our parents, then your peers will begin to define who you are.

Peer pressure is not necessarily confined to your local or immediate surroundings. It can come from our engaging in conversations with different kinds of people, entertaining other cultures and lifestyles, viewing activities on television or the internet. Therefore, the pressure is not limited to your daily interaction with people in your same age bracket. Pressure comes from all around us.

We cannot avoid the effects that our environment and social surroundings play in our development as human beings. This may become productive or unproductive. This is especially true when we are beginning to understand life and how we fit in or want to fit in. No one really knows all the effects of images, situations, environments have on the human mind and emotions. Each of us is unique and the same events have different effects/pressure on different people. One can just be around them and they can have an affect your mind.

It has been said that peer pressure is necessary to our personal social development. It gives us a look or an insight to different behaviors of different people. It shows us the affect that these influences can have on us and the direction they can take us…whether it is an individual affect or group affect. If this statement is true, then who guards or monitors the effects that peer pressure can have on any individual? For children, this guardianship should come from their parents and/or any responsible adult who has a direct bearing on that child's life and their future. For adults, it is anyone who sincerely cares about the individual and who is part of their immediate concern. Peer pressure will test your character. Or, it will help you to define/refine your character.

**Adult Peer Pressure:** Peer pressure is not limited to the youth or the adolescent stages of life. Young adults and older adults are also subject to peer pressure. It may not be as pronounced as in children, but nevertheless it does exist. Adults oftentimes want to give that term "peer pressure" to young people. But in reality, peer pressure is "alive and well" in the adult world. As the definition states, it's the "social pressure by members of one's peer group". Peer groups exist at all age levels. The expression; *"Keeping up with the Jones's"* is a prime example of adult peer pressure. When this expression came out, it was dealing with people trying to imitate/copy their neighbors or keeping a lifestyle comparable to their peers. When a neighbor or a peer would upgrade to a new car, a new house, new clothes, they felt compel to do the same. It didn't matter whether they witnessed these changes personally. Just the fact that they heard about them, placed pressure on them to do the same. Those who had already formed a self-identity and were comfortable in their identity did not follow this trend. They had reached a point where they knew who they were inside. Thus, the pressure had minimum effect on their lives and/or lifestyles.

**Other Unequal Pressures:** We relate the word "Peer" to people being similar in age, abilities, in the same environment and/or surroundings. But this can have another meaning and have profound effects on our growing up years. There are other pressures exerted on us other than from our peers. These peers may not be in our same age group but they are in our common environment. These other pressures come from the home. They come from our parents and/or from our much older siblings. Young developing children are first exposed to family adult members in their early years. These adults become their first "Peers" as far as understanding their identity and about life. These are the most influential peers that children have early on. We cannot avoid this inevitability. The overexposure to "adult" ways and/or pressures can rob a child of the youthful innocence in growing up and learning about life. When a child has experienced adult issues, it's very difficult to unlearn these issues. They can't return to being innocent again. Parents/Guardians should be very mindful and try to strike a balance between what their children are exposed to when growing up. The expressions; "let children play with children" and "let adults play with adults" are true. Another expression such as "Keep children out of grown folk's faces" only suggest that parents and/or adults should be careful concerning what conversations they engage in when children are present. Children sometimes become grown too early in life by "hanging" around adults. These are what might be called subtle pressures…pressure by association…trying to be like their parents. These are normal events that take place.

**Conforming:** The adult peer pressures or instructions that come from the home can influence the child's behavior and what he/she may involve themselves in. When the child does not conform to the parent's instructions, there are sometimes consequences. This can also affect the child's direction in life. This may be called "unequal" peer pressure but it is a necessary peer pressure. When adults don't conform to their peer pressure, there may or may not be consequences. It all depends on what they are asked to conform to.

Peer pressure is everywhere. It's in the workplace, the schools, the community, and in every lifestyle. This pressure could be overtly or subtle. The pressure does not promise to be fair and it can come in many forms of expression. For young children experiencing peer pressure, you should discuss this with your parents or a responsible adult in your life. Do not be afraid to talk to your parents and ask questions. Chances are that your parents probably have already experienced the same things.

Children left to themselves can and will be subjected to the many influences around them. Pressure to engage in inappropriate activities such gang membership, sex, drug abuse, and smoking, could be a consequence of this. You should understand that these pressures do not go away. It is how you recognize, how you respond and/or react to this type of pressure that may have good or bad consequences on your life.

We all learn from what we see and don't see. It's a natural course of learning who we are. This is a process. There is no set time when this realization will come when we know who we are as individuals. You can measure the results by the affect that these persons and/or groups have on your life. Not knowing or fully understanding the effects of peer pressure can have disastrous effects on your life. You can unknowingly <u>sow</u> bad seeds towards your intended course direction and possibly your destiny.

***True Story:*** *I met the mother of a young man who had high hopes of working with a CPA firm upon graduation from college. His grades were exceptional in Accounting and Finance. He had already approached the firm and they almost assured him that he would be employed once he graduated. After he graduated, he officially applied for the position. The firm did a background check and the results were unfavorable. Apparently, while he was in High School he was involved in a misdemeanor with his friends and had a police record. The CPA firm subsequently denied him that employment opportunity. He was, of course, very disappointed...knowing that he had the grades, and the ability to do the job. But the peer pressure from his friends (back then) made him yield to the situation at hand, and the results did follow him 4 years later. He now regrets the whole ordeal.*

<u>***Note***</u>: *Certain types of activities can be "<u>expunged</u>" from your background records. You must seek legal counsel on this. If you have had involvements with the law, you should check to see if these records are going to follow you on your journey towards your intended destination before applying for employment opportunities.*

 ## Chapter 6
# Lifestyles

There are lifestyles for the young as well as the old at different levels with variations in all levels. Whether the lifestyle is desirable or not depends on one's prospective or future outlook. It's all relative to what you are looking for. The online reference dictionary defines the word "lifestyle" as:

*"The habits, attitudes, tastes, moral standards, economic level, etc., that together constitute the mode of living of an individual or group"*. Reference.com

*"In sociology, a lifestyle is the way a person lives. A lifestyle is a characteristic bundle of behaviors that makes sense to both others and oneself in a given time and place, including social relations, consumption, entertainment, and dress. The behaviors and practices within lifestyles are a mixture of habits, conventional ways of doing things, and reasoned actions. A lifestyle typically also reflects an individual's attitudes, values or worldview. Therefore, a lifestyle is a means of forging a sense of self and to create cultural symbols that resonate with personal identity"*. Reference.com

You can be born into a lifestyle, grow into a lifestyle, plan a lifestyle, create a lifestyle, or be tossed into a lifestyle. Most of us will fit into one of those descriptions. All of us (right now) are in some kind of a lifestyle. When you are child, most of the time you are not given a choice as to where you live and the lifestyle you have. Your parents make all the initial decisions. Most parents try to provide the best environment and the best lifestyle for their children given their circumstances. Their mindset probably came out of their previous lifestyles and what they experienced. There is usually a commitment or determination to maintain or improve what they currently have. The degree in which they try to maintain or improve their lifestyle can become overwhelming if their means of support is not adequate. Just think about where you are right now. Some of you may not know if your parents are indeed struggling to maintain their present lifestyle. You may be struggling in your own lifestyle.

**Perception of Lifestyles:** Your perception of your current lifestyle or your "projected" lifestyle can determine your direction in life. If you are still a child, then your parents are providing the lifestyle you have right now. You may decide that you want something different later on. If it's a great lifestyle in your opinion, then you may not want to change it. However, if what you see is undesirable, you must either accept what you have or make plans to change it. But one thing you must remember; it is your *parents or guardians* who are providing this lifestyle for you at the moment…whether good or bad. Unless you are working and contributing to the household, they are providing <u>*all*</u> your needs and expenses. They provide your food, clothing, shelter, vehicles, insurances, education, etc. This kind of support <u>*requires*</u> money. Once you reach adulthood and leave home, some of this support may eventually stop and you are left to create a lifestyle for yourself. Your chosen profession or career may determine your type of lifestyle. So, choose wisely.

***True Story:*** *Growing up in the rural areas of South Carolina, I experienced a lifestyle that was common to most people. Most of us tended the farm lands and the crops associated with them. There were also domestic chores involving farm animals, vegetable crops and/or gardens. These chores were necessary and I could not avoid performing these chores. However, my perceptions of this lifestyle told me that this was not the kind of lifestyle that I wanted for myself. I was determined to venture out from this. I saw my parents trying to make ends meet with the family basic needs. Our family never lacked these basic needs but there weren't much more for other things. Other neighboring families could have been experiencing the same situations. But I only knew about my family. This made a lasting impression in my mind as to what I wanted to or didn't want for myself. On the other hand, I saw other families who seemed to be very prosperous in this lifestyle.*

*There was nothing wrong with this lifestyle because it serves a purpose in our nation's economy. Some people are very content with this type of work and the lifestyle that comes with it. But this was not what I wanted for me. With my plans of becoming an Air Force Pilot, I knew that once my career started, this lifestyle would be over. That is exactly what happened. I do not regret my growing up in that lifestyle because it served a purpose in my maturing, my appreciation of the finer things, and my understanding of what it means to do hard work.*

**Addictive Lifestyles:** Lifestyles can become addictive whereas you don't want to change and will do anything to maintain it. Or, it can go the opposite direction; you will do anything to get out. There can be extremes in both directions. There could be consequences associated with these kinds of addictions. Addiction is defined as; *the condition of being habitually or compulsively occupied with or involved in something*. People sometimes resort to criminal means of sustaining or leaving current lifestyles. Illegal drug addiction could be considered as one of these lifestyles. Some people prefer to live in the "fast lanes of society". But it doesn't have to be drugs or living in the fast lanes. It is *anything* that's controlling your mind and/or body…thus dictating your lifestyle. Trying to maintain an "image" that causes undue hardship on yourself and/or family is a serious price to pay. Your mind and/or body can suffer because of these decisions. When your lifestyle becomes a mental and/or physical drain on your body, it's probably a good time to change or re-evaluate where you are. These conditions will sometimes force a change for the sake of health alone. You may need help in overcoming these types of situations.

**Deceptive Lifestyles:** Lifestyles can be very deceiving. You see what you see; but what you see may not be what it appears to be. There may be things not known or things not shown. Unless you are an integral part of that lifestyle, you will never know the whole story or the cost. Don't be deceived by what you may see on television or what appears to be in real life. Some depictions are real and others are not. Where ever you are right now is *your real* lifestyle and that could possibly change. While television lifestyles can inspire you, they also can deceive you. There is much that goes on behind the scene that you may not know about. It's like enjoying a great meal and not knowing all the preparation it took to make that meal. If possible, know as much as you can about that lifestyle before engaging.

**Cost of Lifestyles:** There are costs associated with all lifestyles. There are direct costs and indirect costs. If possible, all costs should be counted or evaluated. These costs could be measured in; (a) the time required, (b) your commitment, (c) physical demands, (d) emotional demands, and (e) the money required to sustain it. Only you can decide how much you are able to endure and how much you are willing to sacrifice in the lifestyle you choose. Personal costs can be high. Moreover, your perception of cost could be different from the next person. It's an individual decision that you make when pursuing. But whatever you decide, it is going to affect you, those around you, and those you involve in your decisions. Others too, could pay a cost because of you. *No man is an island.*

***True Story.*** *I met a young man who had great athletic abilities whereas he was offered a **full 4-year** athletic scholarship at a major university after high school graduation. But at the time of this offer, he was working part time at a local government agency and was enjoying a relatively good lifestyle while still in high school. It was such that he did not want to give up his lifestyle to continue his education with the possibility of a professional career. He* *subsequently <u>refused</u> the offer and remained on his job. He now regrets making that choice because of his addictive lifestyle during the latter part of his high school years. This decision <u>cost</u> him a free college education and the potential of great financial rewards later on in his future.*

Having money seems to be the underlining foundation of all lifestyles. The amount required depends on your chosen lifestyle. Take time to see what your current lifestyle is costing you and those it affects. If the cost is too high, then consider changing whereas you are comfortable in maintaining it. One **good advice** in maintaining any lifestyle is to <u>**live below**</u> what you can sustain financially. Then you will always have a **financial cushion** for unexpected events. You may decide to eliminate certain aspects of that lifestyle and keep the others. Seek help if unable to decide.

Lifestyles are changing every day. There is not a "One lifestyle that fits all". There are endless possibilities. You only must use your imagination. But whatever lifestyle you decide to create or become involved with, you are accountable for your actions and the affect that they have on your surroundings and the people you involve in your decisions. So, choose carefully and never stop reevaluating where you are. Adjustments could be necessary.

Wise investments, financial responsibility and accountability, wise counsel, your attention to your health, can assure you a great lifestyle.

## Which Lifestyle Will You Choose?
## Be Sure To Count The Cost!

## Chapter 7
## Money Matters

**H**aving *money does matter!* Money is the life line in surviving in this natural life. People will often say they don't need a lot of money. However, most people **will not** turn money down if someone gave it to him/her or if they were given an opportunity to make more money. They realize that with more money they may be able enjoy a higher quality/standard of living than they presently have. This statement is subjective because we all have different views and opinions about money. Nevertheless, we all will agree that we need some form of money or skills in exchange for money to support ourselves. We also need basic skills to get started. Almost one million students who start ninth grade each year will not earn a diploma four years later. You must be able to read, write, and understand the English language. These are just the minimum skills needed. You should also understand basic math principles. Acquiring money, keeping money, and understanding money involves math principles. The bigger your financial success picture, the more skills you may need.

**Making Money:** You can improve your financial status in many ways: It may not be in a particular career field. First, you must define *"Financial Success"* as it relates for you. Everyone's definition is not the same. It depends on what you are looking for and the lifestyle you wish to have. In the beginning of this book, you were asked to determine some things in life before you begin. If you have done this, then you should have a picture of what financial success means to you. This may require taking a specific route or a direction "designed for you" to achieve this.

Going to college or trade school is one starting point in achieving a financial status. A college or trade school education gives you a "foundation" to get you started in life. The combined application of what you learn and personal creativity will determine the rest. However, getting a job after your college education is still not guaranteed unless you are in a highly demanded area at the time of graduation. Many new graduates do not have a job, have not started a career, or they are working in a field that is different than the one they sought.

A college education is not the only starting point in achieving financial success in life. Many millionaires and entrepreneurs do not have a college degree. Some were taught through their trials and errors in life. Some have devised or invented products and services that are life changing and have afforded themselves great lifestyles. There are unlimited ways of achieving financial success. Some have developed their gifts and talents early in life and have used them to achieve financial success. For Example: (a) Singer/Actress-Beyoncé Knowles, (2) Actress/Singer-Janet Jackson, and (3) Golfer-Tiger Woods. Many others in all areas of life have achieved great success.

Some careers will never pay high salaries and have minimal salary increases per year. Therefore, your length of time in that career will also determine when your salary may increase. You must weigh these factors too when deciding. If you don't research your career field, you will never know your potential income after a period of years. This could be another factor in deciding whether to pursue a certain career. *(See Career Choices, page 84)*

**Saving & Investing:** Open your eyes and mind to see what is currently around you in terms of financial opportunities. Investment and business opportunities are everywhere. There may be an opportunity for you to get started early. Or, it may be an opportunity to explore after graduation. Adulthood can be very frightening if not adequately prepared to face financial challenges. Securing and maintaining a checking account is a great start in managing your money. Banks are also a great source of information. Get to know your banker and learn how to save and/or invest your money early in life. Time is definitely your *best friend* for long term investing. Seek good counsel before you do. But be sure you seek this type of counsel from those who are making good financial decisions and investments. Sometimes it costs money to make money. Getting sound advice may cost you too. Be open to new ideas and see if there is place where you can start. But the key is not to start until you have some type of knowledge and/or information.

People who have made wise financial decisions, great investments, accumulated wealth, or have become an expert in certain areas of life, will sometimes require a fee for an audience with them. It is called "consultant fees". They frequently use the expression "Time is Money". Their time and advice now comes with a price tag and it may cost you. However, you could initially pay this cost in many ways other than money. It may require a partnership with you, a percentage of the profits, or other things they may deem as payment. If you know someone in those categories above and if this is your interest, then find a way to gain an audience with them. Be prepared to pay and/or listen. It would be well worth the effort. When you take this approach, your time and money becomes valuable because you have invested in yourself.

The right kind of *self-investment* could pay huge dividends in the short term and the long term depending what your goals and objectives are. If one of your goals is real estate investment, then there may be hundreds of opportunities all around you. There are numerous ways to acquire assets. Money is the probably the preferred choice of exchange. If another goal is to invest in businesses or own a business, then seeking good counsel in this area is also important. Opportunities also exist in cyberspace/internet. Use your creativity and imagination.

This is one advice you can always take and use:
**"Save for the Short Team, Invest for the Long Term"**

**The 529 Plan:** Parents can start to invest for their children's college tuition at a very early age. A 529 Plan is a tax-advantaged savings plan designed to encourage saving for future *college costs*. These plans are sponsored by states, state agencies, and educational institutions. However, these plans do vary and parents should check with their individual states to understand their specific requirements. This is definitely a great financial path/plan to college. Families should *start planning now* for their minor children.

Retirement Investing: It is never too early to think about retirement. This point should be emphasized very early in life…preferably after high school graduation and during your early 20's. Our youthfulness oftentimes plays off this term as something we will never get to. It may not seem logical to think about retirement when you are just starting out in life and it may be the farthest thing from your mind. Most of us say and have said that we have time to think about this. So, we will wait until later. "Later" can come much sooner than we think. Those years can "sneak" up upon us and now we are at retirement age…left ONLY with "Hope" and NOT "Preparation".

***True Story:*** *When I was in my early twenties with a promising career as a Pilot and had income to invest, I was approached with this idea of "planning for my retirement". I was shown a sample chart of investing in IRAs with a 6% return. The example also showed two persons **(A&B, both age 22)** and the advantage of investing early on and letting time work for you. Both wanted to have $1 million dollars when they retired. Person A sought a financial adviser and realized that if he started now and invested $2,000 for 6 years, he could achieve that goal. He did just that. He invested a total of $12,000 and stopped at age 28. Person B waited 6 years and started investing at age 28. Person B had to invest $2,000 for 17 years ($34,000) to achieve that same goal. But*

*Person B invested almost 3 times what Person A invested to get the same results.*

This example had my attention for a moment. I had good intentions and I said I had time and will start later. Well, later never came. I should have started and had the discipline to continue as Person A; but I didn't. Life happened and the thought left my mind. I could have been Person **A** in my current financial reality. Even if I had tried to invest (1-3 years), it would have been to my good. Some investing would have been better than no investing. Time was on my side (back then) for long term investing. Now it is not. Time is always a safe risk when you seem to have plenty of it. You can always start over. *But even the presumption of "having time" is still not a guarantee.* I could still achieve that goal of $1million dollars for my retirement but it would be short term large investments with possibly high risks. Older people tend to use more caution when investing. To lose your 'nest egg" or all your savings in the late stages of life can be devastating. Yet this could happen and has happened to many people.

Since most young adults may not be thinking about retirement during their twenties, their **parents** should **invest for them** if possible. Or, help them invest for themselves. It would be a great gift investment that will grow with their age and time. They may not understand this at the time but they will certainly appreciate this in their later stages of life. Get some legal advice as to how to do this. If my parents had seen and understood the example of Person **A** and Person **B**, perhaps they could have persuaded me to invest in myself for my future. I had the financial means to do so. If I had only seen back then what I see now, I would have.

**True Story:** Much later in my life, I did meet a real **Person B**. Person B had a twin brother and both were thinking about having a substantial income during the later stages of their life. Both started off well in life and worked at the same job for a while. Person B developed an interest in financial planning at age **35** and pursued that interest. His twin brother started initially and decided that this was not for him and eventually stop…less than 6 years later. Person B right now, is close to his $1 million dollars in retirement and he is only **52** years old. His twin brother is still struggling with his finances and is somewhat dependent on Person B for his financial wellbeing. Person B overcame the time factor with a determined mindset and kept on investing. He gained a great understanding of investments and he will reach his goal well prior to age 59…along with other normal retirements at age 62.

You can look around you in your current reality and see the <u>need</u> for retirement investing. Those who are older and are living on minimum income or any kind of subsidized care may now have thoughts about what they should have done earlier. These are realities of life that happens every day. But this doesn't have to be your eventual reality. You <u>can prevent</u> this and have a very high quality of life during your senior years of living. But again, this is all relative as to what you want now and what you are expecting in your financial future. If you plan for less, then you will have less. If you plan for more, then you will have more. *Sowing & Reaping*.

**The Stock Market:** Other types of financial investments such as the Stock Market may require specialized skills. Beginners need great advice and direction when entering this arena. There is big money to be made but there are also *great risks* to be taken. Millions have been made in the stock market. Caution is strongly advised before entering. You can gain a lot or lose all in one moment or over a period of time. You should have some knowledge of the industry. This knowledge includes knowing market terminology; trends in economic times; what stocks are safe; what investments are high risks; understanding long term and short-term investments; when to stay in or get out; when to sell, or reinvest; when to move your funds around, etc. These tools are very useful when starting off.

You may not gain this insight until you have been in this arena for a while. There are people who play this market very well and have capitalized on their knowledge and sometimes good luck. There are no guarantees but there are investments that are considered safe risks. When you decide to play it safe, the returns may not be as great but you won't lose much either. A good motto to use when considering investing in the Stock Market is "Don't invest or risk what you *can't* afford to lose". This saying can also apply to more than just financial investments. Consider *diversifying* your investments. In any case, proceed with caution.

You should do research for yourself about these important factors that will affect your life and everyone who is involved with your life. No one can predict the future. But people who seek sound advice will have a very good chance of receiving exactly what they are hoping for. Seek good financial counseling. Get this kind of counseling from those who have proven that they understand this very important area of your life.

# Chapter 8
# Basic Living -Monthly Expenses

Parents are sometimes too busy with their own lives to discuss with their children the amount of money it takes per month to meet and manage household expenses. At some point (age appropriate), this should be done prior to a child leaving the home. If parents are reluctant to discuss all the expenses per month, then talk with the child regarding his/her projected monthly budget if he/she should live alone. Or, if you are the child, then go to your parents or another adult and find out how to manage your income against your monthly expenses. Knowing this fact could possibly change a child's direction in life. It may be an inspiration for them to make life better for themselves. It could also give them an appreciation for what the parents are doing.

Anyone approaching adulthood, entering college, or at college graduation should be aware of what his or her basic living expenses might be per month. The only way to find out is to manually calculate it or use a computer spreadsheet. This result will be the **minimum cash** intake you need to maintain "your desired standard of living" based on your particular lifestyle to be. This includes your rent, car payment, food, utilities, phone service, car insurance, health insurance, entertainment, dining, etc. The results may surprise you. This is assuming you want to live by yourself.

<u>For example</u>: Your projected calculations have shown that you must make at least $2500 **cash** per month to meet your expenses. To have a monthly take home paycheck of $2500 after taxes, you need a job making at least $40,000 per year...assuming an income tax bracket of 25%.

|  | Monthly | Annual (Monthly x 12) | Salary Needed/Year |
|---|---|---|---|
| Cash Needed | $2,500 | $30,000 | $40,000 |

Now the question becomes: "What career profession will pay you $40K per year...starting after college, trade school or just starting life"? A few careers may pay this amount. But that's going to depend on your individual skills/talents, chosen career field, industry timing, and your grades in school. Good grades are a great start towards you getting a good starting salary in any career field. It may not be $40k per year. This increase may come later in that profession. If this is important to you, then find out how long it will take you to reach the $40K per year. Decisions then can be made on which direction to take or to press on. You may need to adjust your "desired" standard of living or make some temporary sacrifices until you reach that goal. For example: Using the bus line instead of having a car, etc.

Microsoft Excel has an online Monthly Budget spreadsheet to help you do the calculations. You can download this spreadsheet to your computer. I **highly encourage** everyone to use this spreadsheet and experiment with different scenarios. If your chosen profession will not afford you the minimum cash intake you need (living alone), then consider changing professions or devising an alternate plan until that profession can support you. It may require you living with your parents or friends for a few years before you can make it on your own. Or, you can take on a part time job until things get better. **THIS IS A REALITY** that young adults should really consider. Your desired income may not come until many years later. But at least you will know.

**Your Home:** They say that having your **own home** is the American dream. However, that may not be your dream for yourself. You may be very comfortable and content living with someone else and sharing the responsibility of that particular dwelling...whether it is an apartment, condo, trailer, or a house. What-ever it is, that is what you now call home. With every dwelling and/or living arrangement comes financial obligations that must be met. Decide how and where you intend to live and how you intend to meet those obligations. Decide what is best for you, have yourself a plan, and make a good effort to carry it out at that plan.

**Meeting Your Expenses:** If you are unable to meet your basic monthly expenses, your life may become very stressful. This is especially true when you are grown and have a desire to do so. However, there are many exceptions to this. Life can be very unfair at times. We could be born or placed in situations beyond our control and may require additional help. There could be physical as well as mental limitations that we must face and accept about our natural bodies, our living arrangements, and/or our environment. These situations exist and will continue to exist. But if you are an able-bodied person and can reasonably think, you should strive to be self-sustaining in whatever area that your situation will allow you to be.

Making mental and physical adjustments to financial situations in a *bad economy* sometimes don't come easy. But circumstances will sometimes, indeed force these adjustments. *Acceptance* of your reality could relieve some of the stress and could also provide an avenue for clearer thoughts. Your *personal resistance* is only a plus when there is a formulated *escape plan* and there are resources to carry out this plan. The key to any survival situation is *adaptation* to your current reality; but keeping your thoughts always on a higher level of existence. Again, there are always exceptions to this rule. It will require a mind-set to break any overpowering mental and/or physical challenge. Keep track of your expenditures. Don't waste your money. Adjust and adapt.

Monthly Living Expenses are common among everyone *but* different for everyone. How you understand and meet these expenses could be a real challenge in your life. Take time to see for yourself before embarking on your journey of individual financial responsibility. But if you are already facing challenges, ask for help in learning what to do. Enroll in a money management course at your local community college if necessary. **Never give up**.

The following chart is just an example of monthly expenses. You <u>owe</u> it to yourself to do your own calculations so **<u>you will know.</u>**

### Sample Monthly Budget

**Monthly Net Income**
Income (1st job) .......................................... $ 1,105
Income (2nd job) ......................................... $ 955
Other Income .............................................. $ 0
**Monthly Net Income Total** ................... $ 2,060

**Monthly Expenses**
Savings ........................................................ $ 100
Mortgage/Rent ............................................ $ 600
Car Payment ............................................... $ 150
Car/Home Insurance ................................... $ 100
Health Insurance ......................................... $ 20
Heating ........................................................ $ 0
Cable/Phone ................................................ $ 100
Electric ........................................................ $ 90
Other ........................................................... $ 100
**Monthly Expenses Total** ....................... $ 1,260

**Monthly Spending Money** ....................... $ 800
(*Monthly Net Income Total* minus *Monthly Expenses Total*)

**Daily Spending Money Goal** .................. $ 27
(*Monthly Spending Money* divided by 30)*

*the average of 30 days in a month is used to simplify your budget

This chart is just an example of possible income and expenses being paid out on a monthly basis. Your expenses could be <u>far more</u> than what is listed in the above chart. If that is the case, then a job/profession with a higher salary will be what you need or have or pursue.

Doing market research before you embark would be the best course of action. But if you are already facing these challenges, then figure out a way to make your status much better. Seeking advice will always be the first step. Be openminded and get advice from those who are in the area you wish to pursue.

## Chapter 9
# Having Credit & Making Debt

Live and Learn **or** Learn then Live? Unfortunately, the first part applies to most of us...we live and then we learn. But wouldn't it be great to **learn first** then live? When we first choose to "live", we can make some serious long-term mistakes in this important aspect of our lives. It's like jumping in water above your head without first knowing how to swim. You should try to stay in the shallow end first and get expert instructions before jumping into deep waters. But you can drown in water just above your nose. So, if you can't breathe, it doesn't matter how deep the water is. You can easily drown in your monthly expenditures. I once saw a sign that read; "Life is Credit". Obviously, the author of the sign is very shortsighted in how he/she perceives life. Life is not just about credit. Credit plays a part in life but it should never define your life. You were not conceived in credit and your life should never be based on your credit profile or any other profile. Let's now talk about how the world sees you as it relates to your credit profile.

When it comes to credit, the world only knows you by your **Social Security Number** (SSN). The world will judge and/or condemn you by this number. You are only known by how well you pay your bills and whether they are paid in a timely manner. The world is not concerned with your personal life or how your bills became late. It doesn't make concessions for divorces, loss of job, medical situations, economic trends, bad financial investments, or your good intentions.  As far as it is concerned, you are just a number in the financial systems of life. It doesn't see a face or understand your heart. All it sees is a number (SSN) assigned to you and the profile of that number. You are rated by credit scores from financial systems such as the Credit Bureaus. Businesses and/or companies that you financially deal with will report your credit amount and bill payment history to these credit bureaus. Equifax, Experian, and Trans Union are the three major credit bureaus. Although these systems were created by people, they don't always play fair. Human emotions and human understanding are replaced by machine thinking and calculations. The system doesn't get reprogrammed for your personal situations. These systems determine your credit score. Scores 700 and above are considered great credit. Many people do have such scores. Identity theft is very real and you can become a target if you have established good/great credit and become careless with your SSN. Therefore, it is **extremely important** that you protect your

SSN. Giving out your SSN online is risky unless you can validate the source. You should not give it out randomly or combine it with other SSNs to obtain credit unless everyone is aware of the risks. If the payments are late or not made, then all SSNs involved in that arrangement are subject to being reported to the credit bureaus. Even parents unadvisedly use their children's SSN to get credit to obtain things. This practice is not good and may cause their children to have credit issues before starting out in life. It may take many years for their children's credit to get better. But it's not just your SSN that needs protection. *Your medical records number, driver's license number, and credit card numbers need Identity Theft Protection too.*

**Identify Theft:** Every two seconds, another American becomes a victim of identity fraud. The number of identity fraud victims jumped to 13.1 million in 2013. Identity fraud occurs when someone's personal information is used to access money, while identity theft is when personal information is accessed, even if it isn't used for financial gain. Other kinds of fraud, including compromised PayPal or eBay accounts and other online accounts, also increased -- with the number of victims of this type of fraud nearly tripling each year.

To protect yourself from fraud, create strong passwords and lock electronic devices like computers and cell phones, change your passwords frequently, monitor your bank accounts and credit card statements regularly, shred personal documents, install security software on your computer and phone and avoid public Wi-Fi connections, if you notice suspicious activity, contact your financial institution immediately -- the sooner you do, the better chance you have of getting your money back. If you receive a data breach notification, place a fraud alert on your credit report so that lenders take extra precautions to make sure anyone applying for credit under your name is actually you. And take advantage of any free credit monitoring service you're offered from a retailer that was hit with a data breach. New York CNNMoney

**Good Credit:** Having good credit is great if you are financially mature and responsible. However, if you are not, then having good credit is just an *open doorway* to incur more debt...thus leading to the possibility of bad credit...if you cannot handle the increased financial obligations. It could become a doorway to financial bondage. Many adults have fallen into this trap over a period of years...particularly young adults. Most are *virgins* concerning credit issues when starting out in life. You become a prime target for companies who will entice you into getting credit or securing credit cards. If not properly advised, you will more than likely succumb to these tempting offers...especially when you're in college. Companies will start you off with a good credit limit and promise to increase it over time if your payments are timely. These initial offers are sometimes very surprising. You may decide to accept 2-3 offers at one time. You immediately look ahead and naturally assume that you can accept these offers and use them wisely. That may or may not happen. It then becomes very easy to charge instead of waiting or paying cash...believing that when you get a job, all this will be taken care of. This type of emotional reasoning is not good. This very dangerous trap can easily hamper your financial future. It can last for years and years to come. In the Bible, it says in Proverbs 22:7 "The rich ruleth over the poor, and the borrower is <u>servant</u> to the lender". This is true today. Nevertheless, these are everyday normal business principles and practices. Whenever you borrow, you agree <u>to</u> and <u>become</u> subject to the terms of the loan...whether it is a credit card purchase, bank loan, or a personal loan. What you need is a thorough understanding before engaging. It would be great if we all could be lenders instead of borrowers.

**Debt & Debt Accumulation:** Debt can and will burden you down. Just ask anyone around you. It can affect everything you do especially when you are unable to manage these debts. Some debts are just normal monthly debts. They are utility bills, rent or mortgage payments, car payments, phone bills, etc. It is very possible to permanently eliminate some of these debts such as a mortgage payments or car payments. Others are reoccurring debts and the amount may vary each month such as utility bills. Even so, if you are unable to manage the reoccurring debts (the shallow end), life can become overwhelming to the point of causing breakup of relationships, apartment/home evictions, repossessing your car, utilities being turn off, losing your job, household turmoil, bill collectors calling, health issues, etc. Some of you may have already experienced this or have seen this happen to people you know.

The largest single debt that you will probably incur at one time is a home mortgage. You could accumulate other debts that may equal your mortgage debt. But the best thing about a mortgage debt is that it can be eliminated if you sell your or remain in until the mortgage period has ended. Most people do not stay in a home for 30 years. Some people do. College or an educational debt can be cumulative over a period of years and this may equal your mortgage debt. Acquiring a business and incurring business debts are other possibilities.

Some **debt crises** are unintentionally **self-inflicted**. You can get so "carried away" with your good credit rating that you carelessly accumulate more debt than you can handle. Consequently, your bill payments may become late because you must postpone paying certain bills to pay others. You may even start paying bills using your **credit cards**. In essence, you are borrowing from the lender. This causes your credit card debt to increase. They also can become late. They call it "Borrowing from Peter to pay Paul." Your credit card debt is probably the most prevalent debt you can have. You can use a credit card to pay for almost anything. It is very  convenient. You may eventually realize that your job or career does not provide enough income to service large amounts of debt. You may be forced to take on part time jobs to make up the difference. If you have a family, this may limit your time at home. If your job or career should have ended abruptly for any unforeseen reasons, the pressure only compounds like interest rates. It's an endless cycle and it doesn't get better. Bankruptcy sometimes is the only option out. However, the law is now making it more difficult to file bankruptcy. But if you do file, even that puts a great blemish on your credit history. Your quality of life really suffers when this condition has seized your lifestyle. This predicament has also been known to cause suicides. But the debt is not what causes the problem. It's the immature accumulation and the improper management of debt that can bring emotional trauma and financial upheavals to your life.

The companies or businesses that you have credit with may be sympathetic to your situation if you have a personal relationship with them. But more than likely, they still will report your debt accumulation and your payment history to the credit bureaus. Your payments may be on time or they can be 30, 60, 90, or 120 days late. Fortunately, late utility bills are not reported unless they have been referred to a collection agency. This is where having credit issues begin to affect your lifestyle and your quality of life. *It's a self-inflicted pain caused by your financial ignorance*. Getting good counsel is the key.

**How much & how long**

Debt crisis and debt management have always been around. Counseling has always been available in each area but most people didn't know they needed this type of intervention before starting out in life. The people that could have given such counsel were probably reluctant because they were head-over-heels in debt and were trying to get out themselves. This is a very sensitive subject because it involves personal judgment and it shows your lack of skills in this area. But unless your background is in financial management, you and much of people lack these skills. The use of common-sense concerning money matters is probably the only thing that has kept many people out of this crisis. Debt crisis could have been prevented **if we only knew back then**. We so easily entered debt and now we sometimes must pay others for counsel to help us get out of debt. Debt and credit counseling is a big business.

I regret not having or seeking good counsel in my youth concerning credit card use and debt accumulation; or having someone who cared enough to constantly advise me about these matters. This kind of advice and your discipline to use that advice is imperative to having a successful financial future. Some businesses *thrive* on *what you don't know* when starting out in life. We risk the well-being of our financial outlook for ourselves and for our family when we don't receive and apply this advice early on.

Debt will become a **strangling monster** if allowed to grow. The more you feed it, the more powerful it becomes. You feed it with your good credit and your careless spending. In fact, debt loves good credit. *Good credit* is debt's best friend and its biggest producer of more debts. They are "hangout buddies". Debt also has other friends and cousins such as: (a) virgins to credit, (b) immaturity, (c) hard headedness, (d) won't take financial advice, (e) Mr./Ms. know-it-all, (f) this is my life, (g) lack of understanding, (h) I will learn it later, (i) I know what I am doing, (j) I can handle these credit cards, (k) I must have this, (l) I like expensive things, (m) I don't like to cook, (n) will buy now pay later, and (o) refusal to learn money principles. All of debts friends and cousins will eventually turn on you and the strangling begins. Don't let the accumulation of large debt put a **"choke hold"** on your life. Since money is the life line in this natural world, the mismanagement of debt can strangle the life out of you and those you love. Overwhelming debt is a silent killer. Before you know, it's upon you and ready to destroy your life. If not periodically checked and managed, it will take control. Having said that, good credit can be good or bad depending on how you understand it and how you apply it to your life. Don't let your good credit make close friends with debt. Their friendship may be good for each other for a season, but never good for you. Debt can make your good credit turn bad. Just ask the people in your life who have experienced this same thing. Let's now discuss bad or poor credit.

**Bad-Poor Credit:** Having bad credit, poor credit, or no credit is a subject that most people don't want to talk about. The fact is that most people do have credit issues or it's not what they would like it to be. It becomes embarrassing when potential lenders ask us about our credit. This scenario applies to those people who have entered adulthood and/or the work force and decided to put their name and/or job as faith in repaying a debt. All this is done with good intentions. But life happens and things do change. We know what brought this condition about in our lives but now you must explain all this to a potential lender. Then we look back and say I should have known better  about getting involved in those situations. The main reason is because we didn't seek wise counsel before we made those financial decisions and now it cost us. High interest rates, large down payments/deposits, and loan denied, are phrases we begin to see and get accustomed to when this happens. This adds to our frustrations in life when you really need credit and get denied. Now you are forced to; (1) accept high interest rates on everything…long term short term, or (2) purchase with cash or not purchase at all. Predatory lenders thrive on your credit condition. When others with good credit get low interest rates, those with fair, poor, or bad credit are forced to accept high interest rates from 13-28%. These lenders know that some things are necessary but now you must pay dearly for it. Even banks will deny you getting a checking account with them because of your credit issues. We live with these conditions all around us. Our quality and standard of living sometimes suffers because of this. Just ask anyone around you if they would share with you about their credit situation.

In our present society, having bad credit will sometimes **deny you employment opportunities**. Some companies will check your credit profile before they offer you employment. Your professional skills may be outstanding, but your credit profile may have been tarnished from previous decisions you've made…thus opportunity denied. They equate your credit as to how well you will do on your job. The two should not be related unless you are applying for a job as a financial counselor. It's their prerogative to decide based on your credit profile whether to employ you or not. Moreover, they may not inform you if they use this as a factor or not. It is illegal for companies to deny you employment because of your race, color, gender, creed, or national origin. However, the law doesn't mention anything about your credit profile. These facts about credit, checking accounts, and employment should be known before starting out in life. But who talks about these things on a regular basis? We just live and function in these conditions the best we can…not knowing that we can formulate a plan to change all this.

Having bad credit is not necessarily a reflection of your character. It's just a reflection of your immaturity or ill-advised financial decisions made early on. On the other hand, your character could have been less than desirable at that time and it did contribute in your wrong financial choices. Hopefully you've gotten wiser since then. However, it was a risk you chose to take when you decided not to listen...whether consciously or subconsciously.

But **not all is lost**. Getting back your good credit rating is very possible. All you need is a carefully devised plan and the discipline to stick to this plan in order to make it happen. It can be done. If this is your current predicament, seek help in devising a plan to restore your credit and use it very wisely from that point on. But when it is restored, do not let this *re-acquired status* define you internally. All you have done is succeeded in informing the financial systems that you can manage your personal debt, thus enabling you (again) to accumulate more debt. You are worth more than a Credit Score to the people that love and care about you. The cycle *can* and will *repeat* itself if not monitored. If you are not careful the financial credit systems will once again *turn on you*. They have *no loyalty* to a great credit score. The loyalty is only as great as long as the score is great and economic times are good. Anyone who has established and lost their credit rating will testify to that.

Market systems can be unpredictable in bad economic times; even with great credit. There is nothing that says institutions should grant you credit even if you have great personal credit and/or great business credit. Other issues may now come into play. Investor's interest must be protected. You become subject to their internal decisions. Moreover, always remember: with financial  decisions come risks, possible credit issues, and other frustrations in many areas of your life. You should take minimal risks when you're young, immature, and/or when funds are low. Weigh each opportunity on its own merits. **Get good financial advice!**

# Where Are You In All This?

Begin Now By Sowing "Good Seeds" of Knowledge, Wisdom & Understanding in All Areas

## Chapter 10
# Seeking Employment

    **S**ince you now realize that having money does matter, now what? How do you get the money you desire or more importantly, the money you need? What do you need to do, given your present skills or skills you hope to obtain? What is your minimum salary requirement? Is there opportunity for growth in a chosen company or career field? Will additional education and/or training enhance your promotion potential? Will the salary offered provide you the ability to support a family? Are you ready for more responsibility other than yourself? Do you have a time frame for major events to take place in your life (i.e. marriage, children, home, etc.)? Do you have a good understanding of what you will need before accepting employment? Do you have *transferrable* skills? Are you *marketable* in more than one area of employment? These important questions should be asked before venturing into the world of financial responsibility and survivability based on your personal goals and desires. Choosing the right company is very important. In addition, your seeking any employment may be based on your current financial needs. Some of you may not need to have a high paying job right now. You may be living with your parents or some other arrangement whereas contributing to the financial upkeep may be a small amount or none at all. Therefore, a part time job may suffice for the moment. Others may be planning larger endeavors whereas making a substantial amount of income is necessary.

**The Job Market:** The job market can change as seasons do. The economy and some industries go through swings in certain market areas. Knowing the market trends can be very helpful when choosing jobs for the long term and short term. You should not get "fixed or stuck" in one area of qualifications. It could seriously limit your employment opportunities. If possible, diversify your qualifications by learning more than one trade and/or have as many marketable skills as possible. Your salary and benefits could reflect this.

Marketable Skills: What are marketable skills? Common marketable skills for most jobs are; (a) communications skills (oral & written), (b) social skills, flexibility, openness to diversity, (c) thinking skills, (d) energy, dedication, integrity, (e) personal development and learning skills, (f) Teamwork, group, interpersonal skills, (g) leadership skills, (h) work-ethic traits, such as drive, stamina, effort, self-motivation, diligence, ambition, initiative, reliability, positive attitude toward work, (i) logic, intelligence, proficiency in field of study, and (j) your ability to follow orders. Possessing these skills can have a tremendous impact when seeking employment along with other considerations such as benefits, salary, and location. Some skills may take time to develop and some may come through life's teaching. Others can be taught. Having a *good* personality, along with these skills, can make a difference in whether you get hired or not. Researching these skills can give you a head start on what most companies are looking for. Stay competitive.

**A 2nd Language:** Learning a second language is almost a **must**. Although this is not a requirement in most cases, but the advantages of learning a second language *far outweighs* the disadvantages of not having one or *two*. You will make yourself even more competitive by acquiring one. You should research and see which one is best for you. It's never too late to start.

**Specialized vs. General Skills:** Specialize skills are only good in specialized areas. There are pros and cons in being specialized. When there is a demand for a specialize skill, compensations could be great. When there is no demand or a low demand, the opposite occurs. Having specialized skills may require you to live in a certain part of the country where those skills are needed or where there is a greater demand. This fact could affect your decision whether or not to pursue these skills.

Having general skills will give you more opportunities for choices. There may be opportunities everywhere. For example; business skills, engineering skills, information technology skills, medical skills, are needed everywhere. These are just a few. Therefore, it is very important when choosing a field of study, to consider what opportunities this choice will give you.

Now that we have considered some of the basic requirements you should possess in seeking employment, let's now discuss what you seek in terms of desired benefits, salary, and location. These three areas require great consideration when venturing out and/or when first starting in life. If you can prioritize these areas, this will help in your decision process.

**(a) Desired Benefits:** One major employment benefit to consider is health insurance. Health insurance could be a major concern or a minor concern. It's a major concern when you have health issues (high blood pressure, diabetes, etc.) or family hereditary health situations. It's a minor concern when you are young and/or healthy. Health insurance is a **"What If"** expense that can be substantial in yearly costs. Therefore, choosing a company that provides good health insurance could be a number one priority for you. Healthy people may forego this until later on in life when they feel they may need it for themselves or for a family. Before ***Health Care Reform*** in 2010, most insurance companies released adult children at age 22 from their parent's health insurance coverage. The age is now 26. Still yet, that adult child is literally on his/her own unless the parents can pay for an extension or the child can afford his/her own insurance. This could get very expensive if there are serious health issues. You must carefully examine and choose what is most important to you and your needs. Some companies may not offer health benefits. Or, offer different levels of health benefits to meet employee personal budgets.

**True Story**: *A close relative started having chronic medical problems during his middle teens. Fortunately, his parents had health insurance and his treatments were covered. At age 22, he was dropped from his parent's insurance but his chronic condition continued. Initially, he could not obtain health insurance for himself. He eventually found an employer that did offer health coverage despite his condition. He is now in his late twenties and has a family of his own. Unfortunately, his medical bills are still accumulating. Although his medical situation was unusual for his age, the health coverage plus out-of-pocket expenses were very high for his parents. He did not cause his health condition but nevertheless it exists…back then and even today. Health insurance is a <u>major</u> concern for him.*

**On October 1, 2013,** *Affordable* Care *Act* has now made health care coverage available for everyone with <u>any</u> pre-existing conditions.

We often neglect to have **Life Insurance** coverage over ourselves and our loved ones. We think about health insurance but having life insurance is just as important. You can have life insurance without being employed. Plus, the cost per month is far less than health premiums at any age. It is also a "what-if" or "just in case" policy. The coverage amount and payouts are for the designated ones you leave behind. Some companies may have plans already in place when first employed. Check the coverage amount. Having a substantial or an adequate amount of coverage has enabled many families to sustain themselves when these untimely events occur. The opposite has also occurred. These are issues to consider.

There are two types of life insurance policies to consider. One is called *Term Life* and the other is *Whole Life*. These polices can be started almost at any age. Premiums for any coverage amount are *lower* when you are young and/or healthy but *much higher* when you are older and/or unhealthy. Higher coverage amount will require higher premiums. There are many variations in the two types of policies so choose the best one for you that fits your needs.

Designate a *beneficiary*. This is an important decision to make and you should seek wise council before deciding. Just *don't fail* to have some type of policy and don't let your monthly premiums lapse. Life insurance companies *will not* pay out to your beneficiaries if this happens. It's a small price to pay for an event that could affect so many lives. Stay abreast of this very important part of your life. Life insurance coverage is almost a "**Must Have**" even without your having health insurance. The un-expectant can happen.

Another benefit to consider is **Pension Plans & 401K Plans**. These types of plans are for *retirement* based on a number of years with a company. This also may determine if one chooses one company over another. These plans will vary from company to company so be sure you know what each plan entails. Some companies will not have a pension plan. Always inquire about this pension option if considering long term employment with any company. Do your own research. It may require monetary investing early on. If it's a good pension plan, it may allow you to stop working before the legal retirement age.

**(b) Desired Salary:** It takes money to live no matter what standard of living you choose or what quality of life you decide to maintain. They both require money earned or given to you by someone. In some cases, income has already been provided to you upon reaching adulthood. This could be an ideal situation but it may cost you in terms of adult maturity and financially responsibility. However, if you have *projected* what your needs might be, you may be able to devise a series of *job stops* in route to your desired income level. It may take various employment positions to qualify for your desired salary one day. Many top executives may have worked various jobs in route to their current position, title, and/or salary. It could have been carefully planned or necessity dictated a career change. If possible, arrange an audience and ask as many questions as possible with people who have done just that. The road to your own personal success salary status may be long or it could be short. It all depends on what is your ideal salary. *Adjustments* to your standard of living may become necessary during the various stages in reaching your goal. Your determination in reaching your desired salary may require personal sacrifices that may affect your family also. If this is the case, then plan very carefully with everyone in mind. Make them aware of the costs associated with your quest.

***True Story;*** *My First Professional Job: I had several jobs stops in the service industry during my tenure in high school and college. But now it was time to have a "real job". I was highly anticipating entering the U.S. Air Force and pilot training upon graduation from college. However, my plans were interrupted. In January of my last semester in college, the Air Force informed the* *pilot candidates that there would be an 11-14 months' delay before entering active duty and pilot training. This was not the best news to hear. I had to begin seeking temporary employment after college so I could support myself and my wife. I was very thankful that my choice of Engineering gave me multiple opportunities in many areas. I started seeking jobs locally and out of state. But the question was what company would hire me for a temporary (one year) job with a military commitment? Most wouldn't. They would if I had given up my military obligation. That was definite not an issue of consideration. But I had to find some type of work. Fortunately, a company out of California specialized in hiring college graduates with military commitments. They offered great benefits and the salary was comparable to my skill level and would afford me the opportunity to take care of myself and my wife. I was somewhat afraid to leave my familiar surroundings. I had not envisioned working in a large city as my first job upon graduation. I was planning for the Air Force. However, life just happened. But my determination, my desire to achieve, my family obligations, and knowing that I was a grown educated man, made me accept the offer of employment. I was hired as an Engineer. I left the company one year later to enter the Air Force and pilot training.*

**(c) Desired Location:** This could also be a primary concern. It could be a permanent or a temporary change of location. Some people will decide not to leave their home area and are very content to remain. They manage to have successful lives and careers. Others may be unprepared and/or not ready for a location change. Both situations could limit job possibilities and/or opportunities. Some people can't wait to venture out from home and explore life. If you are goal "driven", then a change of location is not an issue. You go where you must go to make your dreams come true. All of us will have various reasons and/or concerns as to why we choose to leave or stay in our environment. There are no right or wrong reasons for staying or for leaving. The choices that we make or will make will eventually tell as to whether they were good choices or bad choices for us. We may have to regroup and re-think as we progress in any location. Natural disasters, man-made disasters, economic drought, and job outsourcing may cause us to re-evaluate our location. Again, it all depends on how important this is to you.

**Summary:** Whatever your needs may be, some type of employment is good unless you are physically and/or mentally unable to work. Life just happens. Assessing your needs and careful planning is important in the preparation and implementation process. Adaptation to current trends, being open-minded to jobs available, can help you proceed toward your intended goal and not get discouraged in your present reality. You must decide for yourself or get help in deciding the priority as it relates to your intended lifestyle.

# Where To and What?

# Chapter 11
# Emotional / Mental Preparation For Living Life

Living life in this natural realm can bring on many surprises. So how do we mentally and emotionally prepare ourselves for living life and where does the training and preparation come from? There is no "canned" way that will work for everyone. We all are different and come from various background and cultural diversities. Nevertheless, this aspect of life must be considered and highly emphasized. Mentally planning for education and success in life is great. However, if your emotions or feelings are left untouched or left in an immature state, then sometimes all your career plans are put on hold or delayed because of an emotional crisis or event. We can never deny or neglect our emotions or the affect they have on our lives as we start life or continue to live life. If not properly understood or properly developed, we can live in state of "ups and downs" in all parts of our life.

Ideally, this preparation and training should start at home. But sometimes parents are not emotionally and mentally equipped to handle life and all that life can bring upon them. Therefore, they cannot adequately prepare their children. The child or children are left to whatever he or she can decipher on their own. There are no easy answers and each person reacts or responds differently to situations in their environment. Time seems to be the only true test to see if one is prepared emotionally and mentally to face life. Life events and circumstances come without notice and/or without warning at times. No one can predict the emotional events that will occur in their lives or predict the tragic events that will affect their lives and their future. We all know that a physical death is an event that can be devastating. But an emotional death can be just as devastating. *Death* to a relationship has stopped many people from continuing to live life. Seeking counseling from qualified people lessens the effect of emotional occurrences that will surely come.

Since emotions involves the heart and the mind, giving yourself a chance to first live life as an individual and allowing yourself to grow into adulthood with time, would be one way of lessening the effect of emotional events. Seeking guidance and counseling in all aspects of your life will help also. It doesn't stop things from happening around you but it allows you the opportunity to have someone to lean on or go to for help. We all need help in getting past events that are tragic in nature. Even parents need help with emotional situations. Again, there are no easy answers.

Emotional or mental immaturity is not necessarily defined by age or gender. Older people can react immaturely at times. Being mature or immature is always relative to the given situation at hand. If this is true, then who defines whether the reaction is mature or immature? Again, "time" is the only testament to truly define the given reaction or response. Everyone responds differently to events and situations.

<u>Loss of Employment</u>: This event can be emotionally and mentally devastating when your whole livelihood depends upon your employment. If you are still at home or not yet on your own, then the loss may not be as great. Having backup support from a savings account, from relatives and/or from friends could lessen the effect. But if those backup resources are not in place, then the loss of employment becomes a major and sometimes life changing event. This could affect your entire lifestyle and adjustments may become necessary. Family breakups, loss of relationships, loss of home and property, and mental anxieties are all *possible* results. Again, it's the individual response to these possible results that will determine how he or she proceeds from that point. Some people will just bounce back while others will face very difficult challenges. There is no guarantee of a reaction or response until this situation affects your life.

**A Physical Death:** Most of us would rather not think about the inevitable personal occurrences in life…especially when it comes to the death of a loved one. Sometimes it's even hard to prepare or plan for that outcome due to the thought processes involved. But we all know that these events will surely come. When it comes to a physical death, those who are from large families often wish that their death would come *first* so as not to witness the deaths of the other family members. I've met such a person. But reality says that someone will witness this no matter what size family you have. Close family members experience much grief when these events occur. This process is sometimes dramatic because each member is unique to the family structure.

***True Story****: My mother had serious health issues during the last 15 years of her life. When I was 17 years old, I came home from school and found my mothers in what appeared to be, some severe discomfort. I was the youngest and was very, very close to her. I became very frightened. All I knew back then was to go to my room and get on my knees and pray. In my prayer, I told God that it would be very difficult for me to be without my mother during that time of my life. I heard him say in my spirit that my mother would not die then, but she will die when I turn 30 years old. I remembered saying to myself that I* *have thirteen more years left with my mother. I immediately got up of my knees and told my mother, that she was going to be okay. I didn't tell her everything I believed I heard from God. From that moment, the memory of that prayer left my mind. When I reached my $30^{th}$ birthday in May, my mother died in June. That's when that prayer came back to me, 13 years later. It would have been very difficult if I had remembered that prayer and was counting down the years as I approached my $30^{th}$ birthday. It would have affected my whole emotional well-being. It may have prevented me from fully engaging in my planned career. God kept that prayer from my memory for 13 years.*

*Fortunately, when she passed away, I had already graduated from college, married with children, and was well into my flying career. The lost was devastating to all of us. However, she had prepared all her living children much earlier by talking to us about life and about her eventual death. Even when she did talk about her dying, it was still painful to me but she felt that it had to be said. The lost was great but we all had to move on with our lives. Each one of us has been affected in different ways by our mother's death and our father's death. Depending on how each of us viewed our parents and the individual closeness we shared, the effects did vary. I have seen some of the different effects. But all of us now try to prepare our children in the same way as our mother did for us.*

<u>Loss of a Sibling</u>: *I have now experienced the loss of both parents and eight siblings. But I have also witnessed the effects of the death of my siblings among my siblings. Siblings also become very close to each other and their loss can be just as devastating. We all have experienced things, moments, and situations among each other that we <u>didn't</u> experience with our parents. The pain of death never gets easy. It just becomes bearable with understanding.*

**Preparation:** So how do we prepare mentally and emotionally for living life? Your family, your environment, your personal beliefs, your faith in yourself or God, your understanding of life and the inevitable events to come, having purpose and destiny, is a great start toward your emotional and mental preparation…with time being the final judge of all things. In the meantime, know and understand the things surrounding your life and change the things that are in your power to change.

The expression that people sometimes quote is one great aid in your emotional preparation; *"God grant me the serenity to accept the things I cannot change; courage to change the things I can; and wisdom to know the difference".*

Another author puts it this way: *"Living one day at a time; Enjoying one moment at a time; Accepting hardships as the pathway to peace.... Amen"* Reinhold Niebuhr

There are so many quotes from all walks of life, cultures, belief systems, and faiths as to how we prepare ourselves for these types of occurrences. But no matter what your spiritual or mental persuasion might be, emotional situations and events will surely occur and must be dealt with. Being equipped will sometimes come with age and/or experience. Those who have been equipped should lend their support in areas that relates to them. We may be emotionally and mentally equipped to handle the loss of a job but not emotionally or mentally equipped to handle the loss of a child. Life does not promise to be fair or reasonable. Life itself will surely teach you but it does not always prepare you to face emotional situations. Things just happen.

We all will discover many steps in dealing with and overcoming these types of situations. One of the first steps in helping ourselves is to mentally and emotionally accept these realities of life. It doesn't stop life from happening but it will become more understandable when we embrace this concept. Our mental and emotional outlook affects our very existence in all areas of our lives. Healthy and proper relationships are two of the keys to our mental and emotional well-being.

There are no easy answers or solutions to these inevitable events that will occur in life. They will occur sometimes without warnings. As to why things happen, when things happen, or where things happen, no one really knows. You may sometimes be able to predict certain events by indicators or by some medical determinations. Yet there are also unpredictable variables that will just show up. Certain lifestyles sometimes may have a direct bearing on these situations...whether it's a physical death, emotional death, or any emotional changes in a relationship, etc.  These events need not be dwelled upon but just be made aware of. Life just happens.

## Chapter 12
# Relationships

There are all sorts of relationships. It's too many to mention in this book. Some relationships will have profound and long-term effects on our lives. There are the right kind and the wrong kind of relationships. We should choose the best for us with our intended destination in mind. There could be "right" relationships for us but the "wrong time" to choose them. Example: Marriage could be good for you; but not right now. Relationships need time to develop and/or time to grow. But some relationships, you need to consider letting go. Relationships can be biological, physical, emotional, mental, or the spiritual type.

We sometimes get involved in *ill-advised* relationships for the simple reason that we can "if we choose to". We may get careless in our behaviors and it can cost us dearly...short term and long term. Ill-advised relationships can hamper or change our plans for our future. Not knowing 'who you are" or not having a "direction in life" can cause you to make decisions or take risks that will affect your life for years to come. Let's briefly explore some of the basic types of relationships;

(1) **Parental Relationships:** A parental relationship is the first one you will encounter in your life. Everyone has two parents whether married or not...or together or not. This is your foundational relationship. It can prove to be very important in the eventuality of things to come. It could be good, great, or a bad relationship. The time factor, the events, and situations surrounding your life will determine this outcome. A parental relationship may not be with your biological parents. We may have already experienced that in our lives. We should all desire great relationships with our parents. But this isn't always the case. If it's bad, things do have a way of changing given the proper time and proper nourishment. Some parents are not ready to be parents. It's a big change for new parents and it can affect the relationship with the child. If you are already a young parent, then your life decisions will come early and may require a new direction in achieving your goals and/or dreams.

(2) **Marriage Relationships**: Deciding to get married at an early age can be risky in the short and long term; even if you are already a parent. You can be a parent and not be married. A marriage license only gives you a "**legal**" bind to that person. However, this license does not necessarily bind his/her heart to you. Moreover, it does not guarantee the marriage will last. Many are still

learning life and learning about ourselves when officially declared an adult. Sometimes the status of being "grown" goes to our head and we think we can do anything we want to do. This is a serious error committed by many people.

You should take time to date, meet people, and find out what your *likes* and *dislikes* are before you make a long-term commitment to anyone. As young adults, most haven't seen life or lived life long enough (maturity) to know whom to choose as a lifelong mate/partner. This is an important decision to make. We are still growing up even after we are officially declared "grown" by society. Age and/or immaturity are just two of many reasons why marriages fail. We can possibly eliminate these two by just waiting. Other reasons are; poor communication, financial problems, lack of commitment, dramatic change in priorities, infidelity, etc. If children are a factor, then they become innocent victims of an ill-advised marriage and/or relationship. If you are man, then paying child support up to your children's $18^{th}$ birthday is a reality. Sometimes financing their college education is also part of that support.

(3) **Friends/Family Relationships:** Depending on your direction in life, there could be good friends and bad friends. If you are planning for a career and your friends are not, then they are bad friends in regard to that area of your life. You shouldn't listen to their counsel concerning getting somewhere. You may still keep them as friends but keep them in a limited capacity. Your constantly being in their presence may change your mind about things and/or life. Some friends may have bad habits and their habits may become your habits. *If your friends are going nowhere, why go with them*? You should choose and have friends who are like-minded as you. Some friendships are only meant to last for a season of growth in your life and some will last forever. Family members may not necessarily be your friends. You would think and hope that they should be. They may eventually prove to be your friends as well as your relatives. But each must be weighed on their own merits.

(4) **Adult Relationships:** There are mature adults and immature adults. Age may be a big factor in this. In addition, life's circumstances/situations can also be a factor in determining your maturity level. Each of us is different and our life experiences are different. Men and women mature differently. This area is broad and is very subjective. There are many ramifications associated with this type of relationship. This type of relationship should be on similar maturity levels if you decide to engage. If it's not a "parent-child" relationship, then each level should be about the same. When the relationship is unbalanced, many things can occur. This is a growth and a

developmental process. With adult relationships come adult responsibilities. There can be serious consequences of engaging too early in life. Emotional instabilities can develop. For the sake of learning life principles, you do need someone who is mature in the areas that you are seeking. Know when to seek, who to seek, and how to seek. Again, you should proceed with caution.

(5) **Business Relationships:** This type can start at any time. It can start while you are still a young adult or still in high school. Entrepreneurs sometimes start early in life. To engage in this type of relationship, you should have something to exchange or sell. There is a price of a commodity or service associated with this type of relationship. We should observe and practice good business principles. However, there are also good and bad business relation-  ships. You should determine how it affects you and your desired outcome. If it's bad, consider getting out. If it's a contractual agreement, then legal factors are involved. Read the fine print. Some things may be hidden or not known. This could cost you down the road. If it's a verbal agreement, then personal principles come into play. Enroll in some business classes if you don't understand what you are getting into or ask someone to help you. But in any area of business, always get good counsel before engaging in this type of relationship.

(6) **Spiritual Relationships:** Some would call this the ultimate type and kind of relationship. You can have this type with God or your higher power. It is not based on your natural abilities, gifts, or talents. It deals with the "inner" person and what's best for that person. This type does not see color, gender, race, or nationality. It is very possible to have this type of relationship with people. It may come through divine intervention, or simply by growth and development. This type should always give "life to your inner self". It does not necessarily change your environment but it enables you to face situations that may occur in your environment. This type of relationship will enable you to change your entire life if allowed to grow. It's simply a choice. It gives guidance, counsel, direction, and hope.

(7) **A Relationship with Self:** Having love for oneself is extremely important. If you are unable to love yourself, how can you adequately love someone else? Love should flow from your inner being. It should come from the heart and not the mind. People usually can tell the difference between the two. You should be your own <u>best</u> friend and NOT your own  <u>worst</u> enemy. Love and believe in yourself. Loving yourself will eventually

lead to faith in oneself. Faith in oneself can cover the unfortunate setbacks that may occur in your life. Faith will enable you to keep on believing in you despite all. Faith is a universal principle and is not defined by any religion, race, or denomination. Faith is an inner strength that only you can define. Faith is also a growth process. Life may bring unfortunate challenges and your faith could possibly waver. But by getting the appropriate counsel, it can help strengthened or restore your faith in you.

**Making peace** with your inner self is also part of this self-relationship. An *internal* war is the worst kind to have. *Everywhere you go your war goes with you.* In getting peace for you, it may first require making peace with others. Make peace and be at peace within. Accept yourself for who you are right now…good, bad, or indifferent. Be at peace with yourself and find a way to change if what you see is undesirable.

**Defining Ourselves:** Sometimes it's hard to define who we are inside. We may be a *product* of other people's attitude, wishes, desires, dreams, etc. We could be battling things internally that's not us. It could be someone else's idea of who we are and who they want us to be. A person once said; *"If someone can define you, they can also invalidate you"*. Don't let anyone but you or a God/higher power define you. If people you know haven't defined you, and you won't define yourself, then life will *surely* define you. This process may take time and it could be very painful in figuring out you. Get help in understanding your internal dialogues.

**Summary:** Relationships are very powerful forces. They can and will define all areas of our life. If you just look around in your mind, you can associate this term to everything you can imagine. The level in which these forces are developed will determine the outcome of many events that surrounds you. You should *first* develop a *good* relationship with SELF. When relationships are good, we feel good about ourselves and about life. If relationships are bad, it affects us too. Hope is sometimes lost because it deals with our mind and our heart. But always remember, life is never hopeless. It is only our perception of life and its events that can make it seem hopeless. **Never give up and continue to live on!**

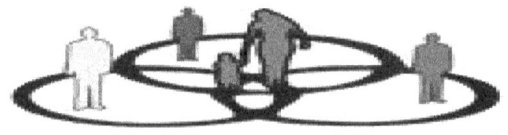

# Chapter 13
# Natural Frustrations

Natural frustrations can come at any time in life. Even an infant experiences natural frustration at times. Everyone goes through these common moments and events. When you are young, you more than likely have "recovery" time to get over these frustrations. Having recovery time does not make the situation any easier. However, just having the "time" is your best medicine. Or, coming to an understanding of what's going on around you…then dealing with it. As adults, we all wish for ample recovery time in all areas of our lives. That luxury may not be given to us. In living life, we will encounter many frustrations. They can come from any direction and in any area. They also may come when we decide to take risks. Some risks are not worth taking. Others are calculated risks. We all will take risks as we continue to live.

There are also **levels of frustrations**: You can be: (a) a little frustrated, (b) somewhat frustrated, or (c) highly frustrated. We can become frustrated by just being around other people. There could be events, a chain of events, natural environments, emotional situations, or just everyday activities that can get us to one of these levels. A person's maturity can make a significant difference as to how we reach any frustration level when these moments come along. Anyone at any time can experience any level of frustration. There also could be a progression of levels. Let's now discuss frustration levels in areas of life that relates to time and age.

Most of our natural frustrations *(later in life)* come from; (a) bad relationships, (b) parenting issues, (c) health issues, (d) financial investments, and (e) the lack of money. At the time of our initial assessments, we normally can't see 25 years down the road because of our inexperience. We press on, living for the present moment and not understanding that time is surely working against us. Our bodies are changing and ever growing older. However, this thought is unimaginable when you are young and in good health. We may say we have plenty of time to get things together so we postpone doing things. We enjoy our energy, our youth…never considering the times ahead of us.

A moment of reality will surely come and you will realize where you are and all that's surrounding your world. Your moment of reality is not necessarily associated with age. It is when you "see and know" for yourself where you are. You could see a bright future. Or, you could see people, things, times, and events that could linger for a while and all the frustrations that will come with each. The *sad truth* about these areas is that you can experience all these at the same time or a combination of each. Let's us now briefly discuss the areas mentioned;

**(a) Relational Frustrations:** No one intentionally plans for a bad marriage or a bad relationship. Yet, it happens all the time. Things seem to deteriorate subtlety or right before your eyes. We wonder how this happened. Or, what we should have seen, known or understood before our involvement. Now it's too late and we become frustrated. These events sometimes create more issues when trying to resolve and/or dissolve these situations. Divorces, separations, misunderstandings, and non-communications are all part of relational frustrations. People have often said to their partner/mate/spouse; "We have been together for all this time and I really don't know you". They have also said; "I woke up to a stranger in my life". By that same token, they could have also awakened to themselves. They don't know themselves. People often become frustrated with themselves for just being human. These are common events. These situations will come and go if lessons are not learned from previous relationships…to include a relationship with self.

**(b) Parenting Frustrations:** Oftentimes we start our family very early in life. When it is planned, we all hope for the very best in years to come. We say we want to be parents and enjoy our own children while we're still young…even while someone is still parenting us. When this happens, our parents *may* inherit the new grandchildren to help raise. This could change their lifestyle too. When parenthood comes un-expectantly, the dynamics of our life also changes. We really don't know the "end results" of being youthful and taking risks while innocent to life issues. The expression "children raising children" or "babies having babies" is so true. We see these lifestyles every day and they continue to be a part of our society.

*Grown children* still living at home can become burdensome to parents especially if the children are not contributing to the household income or upkeep. Grown-up issues come into play when decisions must be made for the sake of keeping the peace in the home. Privacy issues may develop. Tension can increase if there are no clearly defined rules with adults living in close proximity. There should be a plan in place to help the grown children to eventually become independent as much as possible. If not, the situation could become even more frustrating. Compromising and understanding are essential in keeping tensions under control.

**(c) Health Frustrations:** No one desires having health problems whereas simple living becomes unmanageable. You can have health issues very early in life or they could start much later. They could be mental, emotional, and physical issues. Some issues are very obvious and others are not. Some won't be known until some type of examination is performed. Health issues can come through family genetics, from incidences, through human contacts, careless personal behaviors, simple accidents, toxic environments, stressful living situations, relational issues, etc. They may be severe or can become severe if not properly treated. Sometimes you won't know until it's too late. Time frames of certain physical illnesses can be predicted and others can't. Some diseases can come at any time. Some are incurable. Some will linger and could change our standard of living and/or quality of life. Our life can be short-lived by our lack of knowledge or not seeking advice concerning our mental, emotional, and physical health. Our health could affect our living environment and can cause other unrelated issues to develop. There are numerous conditions and situations related to health frustrations. Each of us knows where we are in our frustration level and in our own predicament. Let's now discuss one of many common predicaments:

**Dental Health**: Our Dental Health is sometimes overlooked until the net result of our poor dental hygiene involves getting corrective procedures, which can become very expensive. Regular checkups are strongly advised to determine potential problem areas.

Poor dental health can start in children and adults early in life because of daily diets and sometimes other health issues. There are the known causes and there are unusual causes of dental deterioration. Only a physician can determine the exact cause. Having a good understanding of this invaluable part of our body and our overall good health is one aspect of preventing these frustrations over the short and the long term of living life.

*True Story: My parents experienced dental frustrations as we were growing up. They never told us the full story as to why these frustrations were occurring. These occurrences seemed to be frequent and very painful at times. We saw many "make-shift" remedies being used to relieve the pain. Some remedies were comical and unusual but they worked for all of us. But there were never talks about prevention and what could have been done to avoid this. We now know that daily brushing and flossing should have been but weren't emphasized to us. Lack of Health Insurance and not having regular dental checkups could have resulted in their dental situations and perhaps could have prevented us from having some of the same problems we experience today. If they had known the root cause, they could have shared this with us. Now we are aware of the probable causes of dental frustrations and we pass this knowledge to our children. Plus, we take steps to prevent them from experiencing future problems.*

Healthcare is a billion-dollar industry and most of us will contribute to this industry whether directly or indirectly. There are many other health frustrations that we encounter and will encounter. We should not take our health for granite simply because we are young and/or appear to be in good health. Knowing your body functions, family history, and education on proper dieting and exercising is very important in maintaining good health.

***True Story***: *I met a young man back in the early 70's while he was a teenager in high school. He was involved in many sports and other social activities for his age group. He had great athletic skills and was known for his tenacity to win. He always had a generous heart for people and everyone knew it. However, some of his social activities were ill advised. There wasn't much parental control on his life. His social lifestyle was too active considering his age. Many people cautioned him about the health dangers, the risks, and the distractions associated with his comings and goings. Needless to say, all advice fell on deaf ear and he continued to live a rebellious lifestyle that brought many misgivings to his parents and those in which he involved himself. He once had but overcame an addictive lifestyle of illegal drugs. Criminal activity became one means of sustaining himself. His lifestyle affected many people.*

*But as life would have it, an onset of a disease brought complications to his body which he could not overcome. He encountered many health frustrations during the latter part of his life and died at the age of 49. But he shared with me before he died that he knew how he arrived at that state of being. He made unhealthy choices and should have listen to good advice early on. His risk taking contributed to his condition. He eventually made peace with himself and was trying to spend the rest of his days being as comfortable as possible but still giving back to his family, friends, and the community...A life cut short by unhealthy choices and decisions.*

**(d) Financial Frustrations:** We all should desire a fulfilled life and the completion of our journey. Knowing and fulfilling our purpose and destiny will guarantee this. But even if you don't know your purpose or destiny, acquiring money management and investment skills will ensure a good quality of life and a good standard of living all through your years of living. Money itself is not frustrating. Some people will never be frustrated with money. It could be a mental decision that they make. It's the lack of money when you need it that can make life become very frustrating. When we carelessly acquire material things beyond our financial means with the convenience of 'borrowed" spending, this will eventually add to this frustration.

When we live **at** or **above** our financial capability, this also causes much frustration when things *suddenly change* (car problems, home repairs, medical emergencies, family/friend's situations, etc.). Sometimes there are no "extra" funds to take care of these situations. Our frustration level changes when these events occur. People often say that they are "one paycheck" away from the poor house. This is a common reality for a lot of people. To possibly avoid this, we should make a careful assessment of our financial necessities. Any amount left over will be to our good. It doesn't stop things from happening but we will be more financially prepared when they do.

The following chart shows some areas of the *"end results"* of taking risks early on in your life. These are some causes of our frustrations. Take a careful look. Many folks are in those predicaments today. Just look around you and you will see. If they could go back and change some things, I am sure they would.

| End Result: | Probable Cause / Risk: |
|---|---|
| **Bad Marriage or Relationship** | Wrong choice of mate, partner, or spouse; marrying too soon; not seeking marriage counseling; marrying for the wrong reasons; personal financial unpreparedness; |
| **Still Supporting Adult Children** | Not seeking <u>mature</u> advice on parenting; Not preparing your children to leave the home; not letting go; Being over protective; other health and/or mental issues, other situations; etc. |
| **Health Issues** | Early investment in using cigarettes, drugs, and alcohol; not exercising; not understanding your personal health; not knowing family hereditary issues; unaware of environmental concerns and/or living environments, etc. |
| **Bad Financial Investments** | Too many credit cards, house too big for income size; buying unnecessary things; risky business ventures; no financial counseling. |
| **Not Enough Money** | No early personal investment in ourselves concerning finances; Bad counsel in money matters; Dead end jobs; refusal to change way of thinking; child support payments, etc. |

These are only a few areas that we often take risks or make unwise decisions which lead to our frustration. There are many others. As you can see, many of these areas could possibly be avoided if given the proper consideration and time to understand. Living life is a process that can become overwhelming as we journey along. Having early on good advice in relationships, parenting, health issues, and money matters is "extremely" important. Making wise decisions in all areas can prevent, minimize or eliminate some of the frustrations. In other areas, we won't be able to avoid the frustrations; such as *growing old* and all that comes with that reality.

We may not be able to avoid the emotional ups and downs that may come in life. We may even face breakups of relationships as we live. But we all might agree that if we are financially able to support ourselves and help ourselves in the recovery process (support groups, family support, vacations, etc.), having a *sufficient* amount of money would lessen our financial burdens and would provide some time to heal. *Don't risk <u>not having</u> these financial skills*…for they will surely help you in managing the possible "end results" and the frustrations that come with them. None of us can *turn back* the hands of time or prevent time from moving on. We must learn to <u>*recognize*</u> and <u>*seize*</u> each moment when given to us. That moment may or may not come again. Your moment could be right now.

Frustration with people, situations, and things will surely come. Since we cannot avoid them, the **<u>key</u>** is how you handle these frustrations and how to possibly avoid the "long-term" frustrations.

## Chapter 14
# Have a Vision
# Write Your Vision

**W**hat is a Vision? A vision is a "picture" of what you see for yourself, for others, or for mankind. A vision does not necessarily consist of accomplishing goals or a single event. It may be a combination of many things. It may be an image that you have painted (or seen) for yourself in your mind and heart. That may indeed become your purpose in life. There are man-made visions and there are God-given visions. The dictionary defines the word vision as:

*"The act or power of anticipating that which will or may come to be: prophetic vision; the vision of an entrepreneur"*

*"An experience in which a personage, thing, or event appears vividly or credibly to the mind, although not actually present, often under the influence of a divine or other agency"*

There is no specific time set or known when a vision may appear to you. It can come at any age. When you see it, or hear it, it may even surprise you because of how you may perceive yourself. When you're young, it may be very hard to imagine the lifestyle you desire. There are many, many choices. Most of us have only dreams of being in a particular occupation or in a profession one day. My dreams were to become a pilot, an engineer, and a writer. I was very fortunate to become all three. However, those are only skills and talents that I have acquired so far in my lifetime. I did not have another vision when I had completed all three of my dreams. There was something still missing. Therefore, I began seeking my calling, my purpose, and my destiny in life. I decided to revisit the many things I had seen and done. But they did not give me that permanent "inner fulfillment" that I desired. While in my diligent search, I was divinely given a Vision. It surprised me because it wasn't something that had I envisioned for myself. Even the area that it came in was a surprise. I had been involved in this area but I did not desire it for a lifestyle. Nevertheless, I felt the "calling/touch" in my inner man and decided to see if this was really my calling. *I found out that it was.* There is no doubt in my mind, my heart, or in my spirit about this.

My Calling, Purpose, and Destiny are in *children* and all that surrounds their lives...to include the parents and the community. I discovered that I was still "a child at heart" even in my later years of living. It gives me great joy, that inner peace, and the fulfillment that I've been seeking. I also realize that my innate gifts, my acquired talents/skills will be very helpful in completing this vision. My writing skills are just one example of this. The writing of this book is just one aspect of my giving back to young people, parents, and the community. But this is just the beginning.

However, just having a Vision or receiving a vision is not enough. You must begin to take action on your part so you can eventually walk and live in that vision. In the Bible, it says in Habakkuk:

*Habakkuk 2:2-3. And the LORD answered me, and said,* **Write the Vision** *and make it plain upon tables, that he may run that readeth it. For the vision is yet for an appointed time, but at the end it shall speak, and not lie: though it tarry, wait for it; because it will surely come, it will not tarry.*

I've done just that over a period of many years. This vision is still growing. The more I write the more comes to me. A man once said: *"The preparation for the vision is just as important as the vision itself"*. Preparation will come in many ways, in many forms, and at different times in your life. It has in mine.

Your vision may not be divinely inspired or divinely given. Nevertheless, it's still your vision. *You should write it down* the best way you can. Not everyone is a writer per se. But you still can put your thoughts/ideas on paper...however they come to your mind. You can ask for help in developing your vision. If it's written down, you can review it, analyze it, make changes, and expand it, etc. I've done just that. Writing down thoughts frees up your mind to have other thoughts on what to do. So, take the time to write something and/or have something prepared in place. You never know when your "preparation" will meet an "opportunity" for implementation.

**Being Prepared**: I met a young lady while she was working at a local restaurant. We began to make idle talk about the menu. She saw this book and inquired about it. She read the "foreword" page and said she wanted a copy for herself and for her sister. We started talking about life and her plans for her future. She had great plans for herself and for her young son. She was also a single parent. I asked her if she had written anything down concerning her plans. She said no. It didn't surprise me because most folks have not done this. I hypothetically told her that "I could have been a business investor looking for an opportunity to help someone with their dreams. I could have been just passing through and could make decisions on possible business deals. She would have had great ideas but no plan in place for me to review".

Most business investors will want something to look at before investing. Some don't mind you talking about it to them. The opportunity could have passed her by if I was such a person. She later told me that she would now get busy writing her plans because she meets many different folks in her line of work. You should get started doing the same.

So, what is your Vision? Do you have one for yourself or one for your family? It has been said that if you don't have a vision, then you should attach yourself to someone who does. Lend your support to that cause and/or business. Do your best to help that cause and/or business to succeed. When you do, you could divinely receive a vision or get ideas on what you would like to do in your pursuit of a career, plans, or dreams.

***True Story****: I met a man who shared his quest to accomplish his childhood dream. While he was a child (6 years old), his father had an auto mechanic repair shop. He would spend as much time possible around the shop learning all he could learn by asking questions about everything. Of course, there was school work and other family chores. His father's specialty was auto body work. So, he acquired that skill first. But by him being very inquisitive, he also acquired many other repairing skills (as time progressed) that were associated with that industry. His <u>dream</u> was to have his <u>own house built</u> and to have an <u>auto repair shop</u> in the back of his home. He mentioned how determined he was in accomplishing his dream. There were many distractions he faced along his path but he kept his eyes on his dream. I was standing in his dream when he told me his story.*

By going online, you can find many resources of career information. One source is the U.S. Department of Labor **Occupational Outlook Handbook** (2012-13 Edition). It has information on hundreds of different types of jobs such as teaching, being a lawyer, and nursing. This Occupational Outlook Handbook tells you about: (a) the training and education needed, (b) earnings expected, (c) job prospects, (d) what workers do on the job, and (e) the working conditions.

There is also a U.S. Department of Labor **Career Guide to Industries** with information for dozens of different kinds of industries such as educational services, health care, motor vehicle, and parts manufacturing. the Career Guide to Industries tells you about: (a) occupations in the industry, (b) training and advancement, (c) earnings expected, (d) job prospects, and (e) the working conditions. In addition, it gives you links to information about the job market in each State and more. Visit these informative site links at http://stats.bls.gov/.

Right now, all of us are journeying to somewhere in life. Some already know exactly where they are headed. Others are going in circles or have no definite outlook. This is very common. We talk about wanting to complete our journey in life. A great spiritual leader once said; *"If you don't know what course or path that you are on, how would you know when you have finished?"* Another expression goes like this; *"If you don't know where you are going, then any road will take you there"*. These statements make sense in the natural and spiritual realm. Going to college or trade school may be considered as a segment of a path/course. Once you have passed the required subjects, you get a degree or certificate. You now have completed that segment/part of your journey. But *purpose* and *destiny* may consist of many parts/segments that you must complete to reach the end. Not knowing our purpose and destiny is what sometimes cause confusion and/or misdirection in life. Other occurrences of inevitable events will sometimes compound our search for direction.

However, it's never too late to get started or begin to seek your purpose and destiny in life. If you can clearly define your current path in life, it may lead to a vision…thus purpose and destiny for you. I know my purpose and where my destiny lies. Writing this book is part of my journey towards my destiny. Nevertheless, we all know that in living life, events and circumstances can get you turned around, confused, and/or mislead you. It's about getting the right information when available and understanding what you must do. **What is your Vision? What do you see?**

# Roads travelled
# Paths taken

# But...

Chapter 15
# It Doesn't Have To Be This Way
*"Invest in yourself early-on"*

    Having an open mind, doing research, and seeking wise counsel, can eliminate many frustrations that are sure to come. We must take time to stop, think, ask, and plan. Too many pitfalls could be ahead of you. You also require basic physical needs to live life. Your basic needs are food, clothing, and shelter. How you decide to expand those needs is another matter. Other essential needs are; (a) social, (b) psychological, emotional, etc. Living life has many other issues. Money seems to be a driving force behind much of the issues in life.

    **Starting Life**: Starting your life is like going on a trip in a car. But in this case the car belongs to you and the car **is you**. You may get help in selecting a route to take, but you must eventually be responsible for the car yourself. You must be also careful of the type of passengers (habits) you decide to pick up along the way. Some may want to drive your car and take you to places you don't want to go. Since we cannot choose our race, our culture, our nationality, our  environment, or our gender before we are born, our car could be starting off on a bumpy or smooth road, depending on one's perspective. However, you won't really know or realize this until you learn to differentiate among others. That may take some time. Some will know their starting point and disposition much early in life. Others won't.

    Starting life from the back seat is also not a good place to be. If you start life without the basic preparations, it could be a tough road to travel. The high school diploma is the bare minimum credential necessary to have a fighting chance at successful participation in the workforce or civil society. A diploma may get you to some doors but it may not necessarily get you in some doors. Sixty percent of the *prison population* does not have a high school education. This statistic alone should make you aware of possible consequences when you don't finish High School or have a GED. Other consequences may also await you. Your life is at a starting *disadvantage* when this is not done initially or completed later on in life. Don't let this happen to you. **Stay in school**.

    Starting your life with a family "already in place" could also present some serious challenges when other basic needs have not been met...whether you are

a single parent, or a married/unmarried couple. It not only becomes you that you must take care of, but others too. It could become overwhelming especially when you are young and immature. Both parents are *equally responsible* for the raising and the well-being of that child. It's not impossible to overcome these hurdles and you may require some help. Just don't be afraid to ask for help or get counsel-
ing. There are many young adults in this exact same situation today. It doesn't get any easier if you don't have a plan to overcome this.

**Learning Basic Living Skills**: You might be surprised at the number of people who don't have basic living skills. Some people don't know or haven't been taught these skills. Yet they exist and survive not knowing what they could have acquired. These simple skills can be obtained at any time if you are willing to be taught. There are also levels of learning. Some folks have mastered these skills and others are still working on them. This learning process can increase or stay the same. It's up to the individual.

Can you cook; clean up a room/house; make up a bed; drive a car; mow a lawn; do your own hair; change a car tire; wash dishes; wash clothes; iron clothes; balance a checkbook; manage your money; have personal hygiene skills; etc.? There are many others. Having these basic skills will save you time and money in your life. If you don't have these skills, you will eventually pay others for help. They will make money because of what you don't know. Or, you can live a life below your own acceptable level because of what you haven't learned. You should acquire as many basic life skills before starting on your life's journey. Ask for help from people around you. There is help everywhere for these types of skills.

**Manners:** My mother would always tell me that manners would take me everywhere when my skills won't. Having good manners and respect for others will open many doors that would ordinary be closed to you. I have experienced this personally. Most people are quick to help someone who has good manners and is respectful. They are willing to give someone a chance for that reason alone. However, having bad manners will close many doors when your skills say that you can walk through them. People would privately say that your skills are great but they couldn't work in your presence...thus opportunity denied.

Some people won't tell you that you have bad manners...and some will. They will avoid being in your presence. Comments will be made about you. This may cause you not to receive information, things, money, or even gifts from them. They may eventually say to you; "Your bad manners kept me from giving things to you". Be careful how you speak to people. Having good manners can be taught. It's never too late to learn.

**Dressing Proper & Employment:** There is a time and a place for everything. "When in Rome, do as the Romans do". Being stubborn, hardheaded, and rebellious concerning your dress wear, usually doesn't get you anywhere in life. It only causes people to isolate you. It may even deny you opportunities. These attitudes may be useful in other areas but at the right time and the appropriate situation. However, this should not be the case when it comes to your dress wear. Use common sense and reason when it comes to dressing properly for any occasion.

When you apply for any job, know what is required. First impressions are lasting impressions. Research the company before you apply. Show up ready to go to work. They say you don't get that second chance to make that *first* impression. Don't let the current dress "fad" keep you from being employed. Look your best, be your best, and put your best effort forward. You can do your "own thing" after you leave work if your dress wear is not appropriate for your work environment. Don't take it personally. It is what it is. Know the system. Work the system to your advantage.

**For Men/Young Boys:** Society has cast you into potential leadership roles. You are told to set examples. You are potential heads of household, potential husbands, and fathers to your children. Your upbringing and your environment can be a determining factor in the person you eventually become. Whatever you do or become will affect those who are under your leadership. Others are watching you. A great  responsibility has been placed on you. Regrettably, many of us have not lived up to that responsibility. *Nevertheless, it doesn't have to be that way or stay that way.* Take charge of yourself and your life. Don't be afraid to ask for help in learning how to be a man who is equipped to handle responsibilities. There is no shame in asking. Give and show that respect for your female counterparts. Be responsible for your actions. Have your own mind. Adequately prepare yourself for these potential roles.

Don't add unnecessary responsibilities to your life before you can adequately take care of yourself. (Ex: fathering a child and can't support that child) This support includes more than just providing money. While this activity gives momentary pleasure, it can cost you for years to come...not to mention what is does to the child if you are not ever-present in his/her life. Know and control your hormonal instincts. Be aware of what's involved in this type of activity. Better yet, have enough respect for the both of you not to have a child if neither of you are ready for that responsibility. Become aware of the health risks (AIDS, HIV, STDs, etc.) that may shorten your life when engaging in this activity. Be wise, informed, responsible, and protect both of you. Share this information with your fellow males.

**For Women/Young Girls:** Know and understand your role as a woman or a young lady. Moreover, understand your femininity and how it affects the opposite sex. Have dreams and plans of your own. Don't relinquish your plans for someone else's plan for you. Don't let your hormonal instincts slow you down or stop you from reaching your dreams. Be determined to reach your dreams. You should plan for motherhood if desired. You should plan for marriage if desired. Don't let life or men give you anything that you are not ready to receive. Take control of your destiny. Give yourself enough time to grow up and learn about life. Seek counsel and wisdom from elders. It's never too late to ask for advice. Don't be stubborn and rebellious when it comes to learning about life. What you don't know can cost you.

**For Parents:** You are raising potential husbands/fathers, and wives/mothers for someone else one day. Ask yourself if your child is being equipped for that role. You shouldn't turn them loose and expect things to eventually work out for them. Many mistakes could be made in that process which could hamper or stop their future. Other lives will eventually be affected by your children's upbringing. It's a great responsibility and sometimes the burdens are overwhelming in trying to raise productive children. A
well-known man said; "_It's easy to bend a tree when it is small_". Don't wait until they are grown to try and correct them. Begin to mold their personalities early. It has been said that your children may imitate what you say, but they will <u>model</u> what they see you do. The task is mighty at hand. Give and teach your children as many skills before they leave home. You may not have many skills and/or talents. But nevertheless, all that you do have; show them, tell them, offer them, so that they can be equipped. Living life is about having choices and being prepared to make good choices. Initially, some choices may not be given to us. But when we are given choices, get help in making the right ones.

Single Parents: Single parenting is very common in our society. These are everyday realities that must be dealt with. Some of you may not know how to be parents. You may have been placed in that role because of situations. Some may have been preventable and others were beyond your control. But whatever the reasons; **it is what it is**. Now you are a parent. Get help, get advice, and do the best you can, given your circumstances. There are programs, financial assistance, counseling services, job assistance, etc. These programs are in place to help you in some of the key areas of being a single parent. Take advantage of these programs if you can. But most of all, LOVE YOUR CHILDREN, regardless of anything around you or your current situations. Love them in spite of all. Believe, pray, and have hope.

**Respect For Authority/Parents:** All of us are under some type of authority. We all should respect the positions of the authorities placed over us in our lives...whether it first be our parents, the school teachers, workplace supervisors, or the laws of the land. It's an inner understanding that you know that this is the right thing to do. This basic principle will guide you in many areas of your life. People in author-  ity are not always correct in what they say or do. Nevertheless, you must respect their position as "one of authority". For example: A police officer signaling you to stop by a hand gesture. The person making the gesture is just like you and me. But his position represents the authority of the law of the land and you should obey. Another example: Your parents telling you not to "act out" in school. Your parents are the first authority in your life. But now you also come under the authority of the school system. You may be subject to punishment by both. You suffer consequences when you intentionally disregard the authorities placed in your life. This is an extremely bad habit to get into. Unfortunate situations and circumstances can bring multiple authorities to bear upon your life. This is not a good position to be in.

Don't be "thin skinned" whereas you must challenge everything if it goes against your way of thinking. Learn how to keep your mouth closed and your thoughts to yourself when necessary. Express them only when it's the appropriate time. This applies to the young and the old as well. However, there may be times when you should challenge authorities and some types of authorities must be challenged. When you do challenge those authorities, challenge them with wisdom and understanding...not just from your emotions. Martin Luther King Jr. was a man who challenged the "un-justice" of a system that denied basic human rights and dignity. No matter where we venture in life, we all will be subjected to some type of authority.

**Respect for Elders/Each Other:** How many times has it been said that young people do not respect their elders? Or worst yet, have no respect for each other. Unfortunately, it has been said too many times. If "being respectful" is not taught early in life, it could be a big contributor to this seemingly societal problem. It has been said that if "you give respect, you get respect". And if "you want respect, you give respect". Then who starts the "giving first?" **Why not start with you?** Be man enough or woman enough to give respect to others (especially elders); even if you don't get it in return. It should start somewhere.

Since you may encounter your first elder in your home, then respect should <u>start</u> in the home. But nowadays, even the word "home" can be redefined. Home may not be a desirable place or an atmosphere. Home could be where there is <u>no</u> authority or respect. But whether an elder exists in the home or outside the home, we still cannot avoid interacting with each other no matter where we go. Therefore, having respect, giving respect, and showing respect to everyone as part of our nature can only help us. This too, can be taught.

**Understanding Credit & Debt:** Everyone should be able to; start life, review life, and end life with a basic understanding of the financial systems of this world as it applies to credit and debt. It starts first with the parents having knowledge and children being taught or made to listen and learn. If the parents don't know, let them obtain knowledge. It continues with the young adults assessing their current credit/debt situation and making necessary financial adjustments. It ends when older adults begin to pass down the financial wisdom gained through their years of living life. Credit and debt are powerful forces embedded in our society. They are the fabric of our financial existence. It might be said that the world *evolves on credit and is maintained by debt*. We have empowered these forces to control us. We should begin to take back the power and we control it. It takes knowledge, understanding, and wisdom to make this happen. In the Bible, it says in James 1:5: "If any of you lack wisdom, let him ask of God that giveth to all men liberally". In Proverbs 2:1: "Wise choices will watch over you. Understanding will keep you safe". Therefore, a good understanding of the Credit System, along with the principle of making wise choices, with help you in the natural economy of life.

Everywhere you look people are talking about and trying to get out of debt because of the unwise use of their credit. *In the credit world, "Live and Learn" is not sound advice or wisdom.* Wisdom is the application of knowledge. You should acquire the knowledge and the understanding of this entrapment system and your SSN profile ratings. Credit score ratings are as follows; Excellent Credit 750-850; Good Credit 660-749; Fair Credit 620-659; Poor Credit 400-619. Once you have entered this system under your SSN, you are placed in one of the categories mentioned. You can go from excellent credit to poor credit within a very short time depending how you well you use it. With a <u>good knowledge</u> of this system, credit can work for you to your best interest and debt can be managed. The *immature mixture* of the two will eventually control you.

**The Justice System:** The Justice System is ever present. Do not enter this system the wrong way. Don't become a *victimizer*. Criminal activities, misdemeanors, and juvenile reports can cast a shadow over your life. Depending on the time frame (age) in which these events occur, this shadow (record) may not be so easily removed and can *follow* you to your future. These records can delay or prevent you from obtaining employment or entering into business opportunities. Youthful innocence and/or ignorance to the laws of the land can have a lifelong affect. Hopes, dreams, ideas, and future plans have been "snatched" up by the system just from you being in the wrong place at the wrong time. Always be aware of your surroundings and know what places and activities to avoid. This can also happen when you *knowingly* engage in illegal activities in an attempt to "beat/test" the system. Taking chances for the sake of taking chances can be exciting for the moment but it can cost you unnecessary pain and suffering down the road. Speeding violations (MVR) and DUIs have hampered many who seek employment. Depending on the type of job and/or career desired, some employers will require an extensive background investigation which involves checking the "System" for your name. Your name is found by your Social Security Number.

Whenever there is a situation involving **incarceration** (a social timeout), your life becomes adversely affected and it affects those around you. The loss of employment, loss of relationships, and home or apartment evictions are all possibilities. Even the *frequency* of incarcerations has negative overtones on your life. The type and severity of certain activities can sometimes prevent any attempts of completing your dreams. You can also enter the system when convicted of "involuntary' incidents. False accusations along with false convictions will have the same affect. Your lifestyle instantly changes and is now dictated by the State for a period of time. The system is not perfect and mistakes have been made…. **But**

The Justice System is necessary for a reason. It works for the betterment of our society. It is there to protect you and to hold you accountable for your actions. Law abiding citizens need not fear this system. But you *can* get "trapped" or "caught up" in the system. No path into the system is ideal but life does happen. You should *never lose hope* if this is your situation. Many people still become very productive and still contribute immensely to society. Well known people from many walks of life have experienced this path. Some have learned invaluable lessons and are now instructing others on "how to" avoid the system. Take heed how you manage your life.

**Distractions in Life:** There are many distractions in life. There are social distractions, emotional distractions, and physical distractions. Some have far reaching affects. These distractions can delay, change, or stop any "well thought out" plans. Distractions also include involvement in dangerous activities such as; (a) gang membership, (b) criminal activity, (c) illegal drug use, and (d) alcohol and/or substance abuse, etc. These activities will only jeopardize or destroy your life and possibly those around you. Dropping out of school can lead to these kinds of activities. You could become a burden to society. **Substance abuse** can affect the seeds of unborn generations that exist within all of us.

Other subtle but very ***significant distractions*** are; watching TV, gaming, surfing the net, cell phone usage, texting, hanging out, too active social life, etc. Social Medias to include Facebook, Twitter, Myspace, YouTube, etc., could also be distractive. While these are normal activities, it is the over indulgence and the excessive involvement that *may* become *addictive*. These normal everyday distractions can consume much of your time. You should weigh the pros and the cons before spending a lot a time in these activities.

You should become aware of these distractive forces that will seize control of your mind and body...lasting for years and sometimes even unto death. Being focused on an objective/goal and having a well-balanced lifestyle in spirit, soul, & body will help prevent this. You should always know what things and/or people that are *influencing your thought life*. Eliminate all the bad people and/or things and keep only the good ones. Make the best out of your moment of reality. Don't become part of a *bad* statistic and don't let life control you. Be in charge of your own destiny.

**The Reality of Your Moment:** Where ever you are right now in life is your *reality*. Despite what it may look like, or appear to be, or how you wish it to be, **it is what it is**. Take a good look at it and decide if you are happy with your current reality. If not, do you have a plan to change it? We all should ask ourselves that question. I dealt with the reality of my moment back in the "60-70's concerning my physical size in regards to playing sports in high school and the color of my skin in regards to flying airplanes. It was very real. I did not deny the reality of my moment. It was what it was. Nevertheless, my mind, my goals, and my dreams kept me above my environment surroundings, my physical limitations, and the color of my skin. The reality of my moment <u>did not</u> define what I wanted to do or the person I wanted to become. I pressed on to achieve my goals and dreams. I remain focused on what I had to do and I was determined to do the best I could in trying to reach my goal. So, what is the reality of your moment? If your current reality is undesirable, then are your dreams and plans keeping you above it?

It has been said; "*So as a man thinketh, so is he*". It has also been said that "a mind is a terrible thing to waste". Many Scientists say that we only use 10% of our brain. If man has accomplished so much using only 10 percent of his brain; imagine using 15%? You can literally change your character by changing your thought life. Thoughts are the foundation of all manifested things...good and bad. So, what do you often think about? Your thoughts, your dreams, and your goals can help transcend your reality. It did for me...so can yours. Whatever you feed your thought life is what you *may* become. Learn to recognize the distractive influences on your mind. Therefore, let your good thoughts begin to transcend your present reality.

**Summary:** It doesn't have to be this/that way in your life. You can learn some things right now. Don't let life pass you by without trying to find your purpose and destiny. It may require a diligent search on your part. Don't let it be said that you didn't try...especially if you mentally and physically able to do so. Don't let your dreams end up in the graveyard of unfulfilled dreams. *"Ask, and it shall be given unto you; Seek, and you shall find; Knock, and the door will be opened unto you"*. You should never stop asking, never stop seeking, and never stop knocking. You may never know what fulfillment lies ahead. **The time is NOW.**

**Guard Your Life with Wisdom & Understanding**

# Chapter 16
# My Sowing & Reaping
# Seedtime & Harvest - Karma
*Universal Principles Worth Understanding Early*

**U**nderstanding these two universal principles can bring results in the positive or negative in your life. If you are fortunate to understand these principles early on, then your life will have *your* desired outcomes. Whatever kind of seed you sow *(plant)* in thought, word or deed, it will produce fruits (results) of the same kind...whether that seed was sown intentionally or unintentionally. These *principles will work* in any lifestyle, any environment, and in any intended direction or purpose. For simplicity, I will use a *farming lifestyle* to explain these two principles with reference to the bible.

*Gen 1:11-12 And God said, Let the earth bring forth grass, the herb yielding seed, and the fruit tree yielding fruit after his kind, whose <u>seed is in itself</u>, upon the earth: and it was so. And the earth brought forth grass and herb yielding <u>seed after his kind</u>, and the tree yielding fruit, whose seed was in itself, after his kind: and God saw that it was good. Gen 8:22 While the earth remaineth, <u>seedtime and harvest</u>, and cold and heat, and summer and winter, and day and night <u>shall not</u> cease. (KJV)*

*Galatians 6:7 Be not deceived; God is not mocked: for whatsoever a man soweth, that shall he also reap.*

**My Limited Knowledge & Understandings**: In my understanding of *Sowing & Reaping*, I was somewhat aware of this principle early on but didn't give it much thought until a much "<u>Lived Life</u>" has shown me the path that I took and the results received. I use to associate "sowing and reaping" as having "only" negative results based on *my* sowing alone. Now I realized that some of my reaping could have been because of me and some because of the sowing of other people and/or entities. You could be the victim of "other" people's sowing and reaping. All of us are constantly sowing and reaping; even in the smallest things of life.

*"Sow a <u>thought</u> reap a habit; sow a <u>habit</u> reap a character; sow a <u>character</u> reap a destiny"*. Stephen Covey

By default, we initially reap *everything* that has been sown into our environment...beginning at birth. These are the results of *other people/entities, sowing seeds*...whether the seeds are personal, social, and/or political. In the most personal sense, you are the *result* of your father sowing a personal biological seed. But you can only determine the results of your environmental and/or personal reapings by comparison as you get older or by someone showing you the differences. If your reaping has been positive, then great. If not, then you must begin to re-sow your own seeds into your own destiny by obtaining prior knowledge and understanding of the lifestyle you are seeking. Seek help *first* in sowing when you don't fully understand.

In my understanding of *"seedtime & harvest"*, even though I grew up on a farm, the term was never explained to me. This principle was ever-present and was always at work in my environment; *the planting of **one** seed of corn in the earth grew a stock of corn with many ears of corn; the planting of **one** watermelon seed grew a vine that produced many melons with many seeds*; The planting of any seeds will reap a harvest in their own season. Seeds will always multiply themselves when planted in good soil. But the key to having a successful a harvest is *"knowing what time to plant* and *understanding* what soil (areas) to plant your seeds of *thoughts, words, deeds, time, and money into*. If the chosen soil is *not fertile*, then your seeds will not have the desired harvest. My father would always till (understand) the soil before planting (sowing). And he knew the time when to expect a harvest. When I asked my mother about my choice to become a pilot, my mother sowed (planted) thoughts in my mind by telling me that I could *do anything* I wanted to do just by *trusting in God and believing in myself*. Her thoughts were powerful thoughts planted in good soil (me). Those thoughts took root and my career/destiny is the result thereof. (My Harvest)

All through this book I've shown the results my personal choices/decisions and the *possible results* (Karma) of your personal choices and/or decisions. These choices and decisions start during our childhood and they continue throughout our lifetime. Some *results can be predicted* if we plant (sow) with understanding. Others are unpredictable when we plant (sow) *without* understanding. The results will *still come,* whether they are good or bad. It is always good to have prior knowledge in the intended direction *before* making any decision or embarking on your journey in life. As you can see in certain areas of my life, my decisions and choices produced positive results. And in some other areas, I did not seek or heeded the knowledge I'd received and I reaped the consequence of those choices and decisions.

*Proverbs 4:7 <u>Wisdom</u> is the principal thing; therefore, get wisdom: and with all thy getting <u>get understanding</u>.*

**Personal Choices & Decisions:** The following areas are the results of these seed principles that I knowingly and unknowingly applied in my life. I <u>now</u> know how these principles could have had a more profound effect on the positive side if I had a better understanding early on. I will show you true examples of these principles based on *my* past lifestyle, present, and my future direction.

**1. Career Profession:** In my quest to become an ***Air Force Pilot***, I *sowed* into myself knowledge of the requirements and guided myself into being in a position to become one. The requirements were: a high school diploma, college graduate, physical requirements, social behaviors, etc. I remained focused towards my quest and I *reaped* the rewards becoming an Air Force Pilot and with all the benefits, privileges. I also reaped the rewards of now being a Veteran with short/long term educational, financial, and medical benefits, etc. This applies to all branches of service. With regards to having a good backup job profession when my flying career ended, I *sowed* into myself by getting a degree in ***Electrical Engineering*** and *reaped* the benefits of securing a *federal civil service* profession which allowed me to retire with a <u>pension</u> and other lifetime benefits. In my quest to <u>continue</u> *traveling* and seeing the world, I *sowed* into myself by being employed in the ***Airline Industry*** and now *reaping* the benefits of retirement with *lifetime* flying privileges. Out of curiosity sake, I took a ***typing course*** in high school. This one particular skill is still producing huge results in my life. It has helped me to write more easily…not to mention other areas that typing skills are a must have. There are countless others.

**2. Financial Preparation/Investments:** With all my miscalculations and/or ill-advised decisions and choices made in living my life, I **regret** not following the example (Persons A&B) mentioned in *Chapter 7: Money Matters*. If I had chosen to pursue that plan and sowed into my financial future, my current situation would have been much better. Because of my thinking that I had time to decide, that mindset became my demise. My chapter on *Chapter 9: Having Credit and Making Debt* was the "<u>after the fact</u>" consequences of <u>not</u> learning before I started living. These two chapters should be read/re-read and understood thoroughly. But even now looking back at my miscalculations, I now understand that if those miscalculations and/or missteps had not occurred, I could not have gained the knowledge and the wisdom that I now share in this book.

**3. My Personal Relationships:** I have sown seeds in my personal life that have also produced desired and undesired results. This was another area that I should have sought wise counsel before engaging. I got married in college.

(**Not recommended**). I did not know that I needed more time to grow up as man and needed time to *first* understand me. I could not provide for myself back then, let alone trying to provide for a wife. But getting married was not the issue. The institute of marriage is great. In my decision to start a family early, I sowed lack of knowledge, wisdom, and understanding in this very important aspect of my life. When *I didn't know, and didn't ask*, the results did follow. The positive results were; I have two beautiful children who I love very much. The negative results were; *not knowing how to be a man, a husband, or a father* during this early stage of my life. In this instance, my entire family reaped the results of my sowing a lack of understanding. My children reaped the results of an unstable marriage and household. Not only did my immediate family reaped, but everyone involved directly in our lives and around us reaped also. Growing up in all three areas (at the same time) was not easy and I reaped the results in all three. I needed guidance in all three before engaging. But I have since understood what I sowed and I'm now reaping all positive results in my new understanding of parenting. As I mentioned in my *Foreword*, my lack of knowledge in finances and relationships have cost me in living my life. But I've gain so much in the understanding of the two that I can write with understanding about them both. Lessons learned and Experience gained. *"In all my getting, I did get understanding".*

**4. Spiritual Development/Growth:** In my travels since college graduation, my lifestyle creations took me to other places where I was opened to see and learn new philosophies/doctrines of living life. I found a place (good soil) where my spirit man could grow and has grown. Over 20 years I have planted myself into a church ministry. The resultant growth has been extraordinary. Out of this ministry, I have reaped a Vision for my next career involvement. This ministry has cultivated my mine, heart, and spirit.

*Proverbs 29:18 Where there is no vision, the people perish: ...*

*Habakkuk 2:2 And the LORD answered me, and said, Write the vision, and make it plain upon tables, that he may run that readeth it.*

I have traveled many roads in route towards my purpose and destiny. Some roads were very rough because of choices and decisions I made. Those roads are now considered as learning and growing experiences which led me to the writing of this book for children and young adults. I know now that they were necessary in my preparation on this journey. We can make some of our roads much easier if we listen first. The time **is NOW**.

# Chapter 17
##  A Great Seed Planter – SGM Brown

Word seed planting in children initially begins with the biological parents or whoever will have a direct responsibility over that child. Overtime, this could be many individuals and/or entities. A child will receive "word" seeds from many people when he/she is growing up. These are inevitable situations that we all face throughout our lives. When we come to understand these principles of planting seeds, then we now should plant with knowledge and wisdom. This will often take some time to acquire this state of being. My parents, my siblings, and my environment were my *first* initial seed planters. Teachers are probably the next crucial step in life's learning process. We **all are teachers** by what we say and do. *And we all <u>sow</u> seeds by what we say and do*. It is that wisdom gained in our actions and interactions that should <u>inspire</u> us to share that wisdom and understanding with others. When we do, we then become seed planters. There are good seeds planters as well as bad seeds planters. Only time will determine what harvest crops will be produced as the result of our sowing seeds. The result will be a harvest of whatever we've sown. But this story is about a seed planter that I know personally.

**Great Story: Sergeant Major Brown** has become a true a seed planter. Over his years of living and experiencing life, he has gained much wisdom and understanding that he *continues* to pass it along to the many people he has come to know. He may be known as the "Giver" to the many individuals/families that have had the opportunity to be in his presence for a period of time. He gives of himself in words and in deeds. As my elder brother, he has given to me as a parent, a brother, and as a friend with a caring and loving heart. But not just with me, he gives with that same compassionate spirit to everyone that he has a chance to impart himself. I say this about him, because I don't know anyone personally that gives like this. My mother Minnie, of course, was the first and my sister Minnie is another example of this. Since our professional paths have taken us in different directions, the commonality is our bloodline and the coming up under the giving and compassionate spirit of our mother. This alone, was the beginning of our foundation that all of us inherited from our mother.

As a Junior High School ROTC teacher, a community leader, a participant in local church activities, a mentor to both children and adults, he is well respected and loved in the community. Those who know him personally have only great words to say about him. He has planted so many seeds into so many lives that he is reaping a great harvest by those returning to say to him *"Thank you for planting those thoughts in me when..."* These individuals have gone on to become productive citizens in our society. They have now become seed planters by what they have received and witnessed from Sergeant Major Brown. They have also returned (unannounced) to the school in which they sat under his teachings to share with his current students. They now emphasized the importance of his teachings and how their lives have been affected since they first met him. But this is not just limited to his former students; many others are saying the same words by this remarkable man. They too, are making a difference in the lives of people that they now meet because of Sergeant Major Brown.

Sergeant Major Brown has also distinguished himself by achieving one of highest rank among his former enlisted peers in the U.S. Army. He also made the *prestigious* Command Sergeant <u>Selectee List.</u> He had to *refuse* the appointment because it required an overseas assignment when a family member's illness *required* his physical presence during that time; denying himself for the sake of others. He has achieved many other awards in recognition for outstanding performances and services to our country as a soldier. He has accomplished so many noteworthy things that are too numerous to mention in this book. When speaking to him, he is very humble in his giving and kind spirit. He is a man of life-giving principles that people have come to know. He is still planting good seeds of wisdom, knowledge, and understanding. He has also planted good seeds in his own personal life by *first*, getting an education and pursuing a path of education and knowledge along with his many accomplishments in life. He now personally reaps great benefits from his own seeds sown many years ago. Time has given him *great* short term and long-term results in many areas of his life; to include successful children.

Seed planters are everywhere. Some are well known and famous for their giving spirit. Presidents, authors, celebrities of all kinds, are examples of this. These are all great people. But how many of you know them personally? Some of you may know many such individuals as my brother. There may be such individuals in your community…in your **home**. They will make an impact <u>in</u> your life, and <u>on</u> your life in some form or fashion. They will plant seeds knowingly and unknowingly. The results may not be known for years. Someone took time and sowed seeds into President Barack Obama all during his life. And now he is sowing seeds into others. He is great man to admire.

 But nevertheless, this *brief* chapter is to *Honor* Sergeant Major Brown for the seeds he has sown into my life and to recognize the seeds he has sown into the lives of so many others. *So as brother to brother;* Sergeant Major Brown, **"I Salute You"**.

# What Seeds Are You Planting And Into Whom?

# Who Are You Influencing In Your Surroundings?

Chapter 18
# THE TIME CLOCK
### "Working For Us or Against Us"

Depending on what your goals and objectives are, the Time Clock can work for you or against you. Right now, you could be working against the clock in your current reality. If we as individuals don't realize or see a need to plan, then the Time Clock will work its affects however it wills on all the above areas. Then we will look back but can't go back. All of the areas above may be interrelated for you and may need prioritizing. Only you can decide the order as it relates to your intended lifestyle and direction.

But no matter what area becomes your main focus, each one is a function of time and/or age. Even longevity is not guaranteed. Wherever you are, your moment is now. The Time Clock doesn't stop ticking just because you *stop* planning. Don't let time get the best of you or stop you. The sooner you understand this, the better off you will be. Know when, how, and where to use your time. Time is your most precious gift. When yours runs out, it can affect more than just you. Use your time wisely.

# "TICK TOCK - TICK TOCK"

**Who or What Is To Blame?** If you have read this entire book, I am sure you can see; (a) where you started from, (b) where you are right now, and (c) where you might be headed. Some of us will cast blame on our background, our gender, our environment, our race, our education, our ignorance, and even on our parents as to how we got to this point in our lives. There may be blame in all areas.
But we cannot go back and undo things. It **"was what it was"** and now **"it is what it is"**. When and if we do look back, we may remember instances where we could have turned things around or gone in a different direction if we had listened; but we didn't. Someone did try to sow seeds in our lives at some point but our minds and hearts may have not been ready to receive them. The decisions made, directions taken, and paths chosen may not have proven as productive or prosperous as we had hoped; and now we are here. However, some decisions, directions, and paths did prove very productive. Whether it is good or bad, now we must live with our current reality **or** begin to change it. It's still a choice to make.

If by chance you are just starting in life, you now have this wisdom to guide you. If you are in the middle stages or late stages of life, there still may be time to make some adjustments. The areas mentioned throughout this book may be simplistic and fundamental. Nevertheless, they are real. They are the everyday situations in life. They are the basic foundational keys in becoming well-rounded adults. Somehow, we may have strayed away from and/or have forgotten these basic living principles. Having this fundamental knowledge of living principles will always pay huge dividends in all areas of your life. Learning these principles and applying these keys early on can only make life very productive in any area that you choose to venture. *You are living and writing your own life's story*. Something *will be said about* you at the end of your life. Make sure that it's what you want said about you. Take time to become knowledgeable in the areas and issues that will affect you and your world. Always strive to make life better for yourself and for others around you.

Begin your life with the end in mind...
Stop, Listen, and Learn.

Chapter 19
# Statistics to Consider

- Chronic diseases are long-term illnesses that are rarely cured. Chronic diseases such as heart disease, stroke, cancer, and diabetes are among the most common and costly health conditions. Chronic health conditions negatively affect quality of life. Many chronic conditions can be prevented or modified with behavioral interventions.

- Smoking has serious long-term consequences, including the risk of smoking-related diseases and the risk of premature death, as well as increased health care costs associated with treating the illnesses. Many adults who are currently addicted to tobacco began smoking as adolescents, and it is estimated that more than 5 million of today's underage smokers will die of tobacco-related illnesses.

- Dropouts from high school are more likely to be unemployed and earn less when they are employed than those who complete high school.

- In an average week during the 2006 school year, about 8 percent of youth ages 16–19 were neither enrolled in school nor working.

- The teen birth rate in the United States rose in 2006 for the first time since 1991, and unmarried child bearing also rose significantly, according to preliminary birth statistics.

- By age 30, three-quarters of women in the U.S. have been married and about half have cohabited outside of marriage.

- 8.9 percent of persons 15–44 years of age had engaged in sexual behaviors in the past year that put them at increased risk of HIV, and 1.5 percent had engaged in drug use behaviors that put them at risk. In all, an estimated 9.9 percent engaged in either drug use or sexual behavior that placed them at increased risk for HIV. Including those who were treated for a sexually transmitted disease (STD) in the past year.

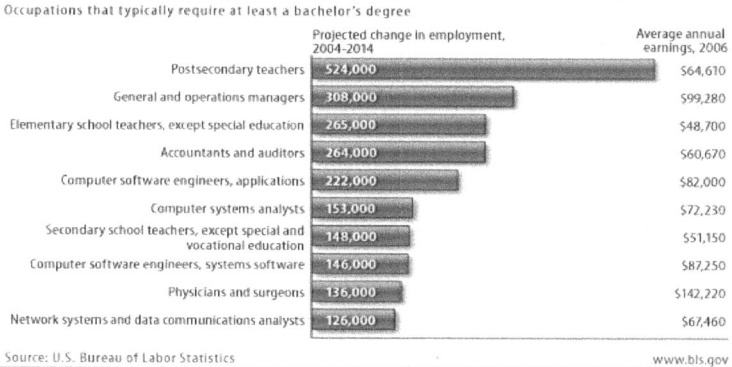

Excerpts/data taken from:
Report: CDC October 2008, Agingstats.gov,
Institute of Education Sciences U.S. Department of Education National Center for Education Statistics; U.S. Department of Labor Bureau

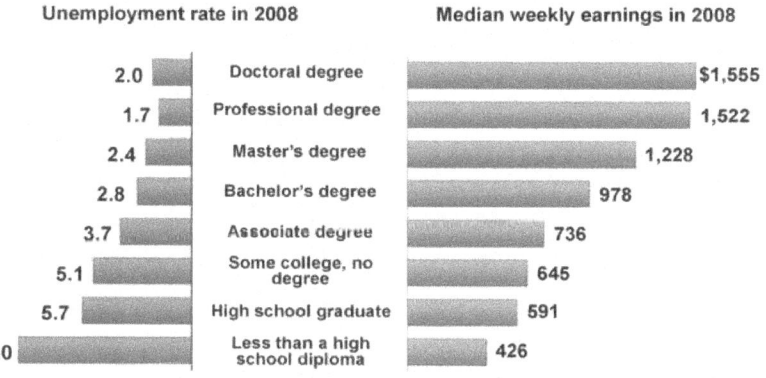

| Student Athletes | Men's Basketball | Women's Basketball | Football | Baseball | Men's Ice Hockey | Men's Soccer |
|---|---|---|---|---|---|---|
| % High School to College | 2.9% | 3.15 | 5.8% | 5.6% | 12.9% | 5.7% |
| % College to Pro | 1.3% | 1.0% | 2.0% | 10.5% | 4.1% | 1.9% |
| % High School to Pro | .03% | .02% | .09% | .5% | .4% | .08% |

**%High School Players Who Get The Chance To Go Pro.**

**Source:** National Collegiate Athletic Association (NCAA). Estimated Probability of Competing in Athletics beyond the High School Interscholastic Level

Chapter 20
## SUGGESTED CAREER CHOICES

The following pages are potential Career Choices based on:

# PERSONALITY & ENVIRONMENTAL DESCRIPTIONS

*IF YOU ARE...*

A. REALISTIC
B. INVESTIGATIVE
C. ARTISTIC
D. SOCIAL
E. ENTERPRISING
F. CONVENTIONAL

# REALISTIC

## PERSON AND ENVIRONMENT DESRCIPTION

### Realistic Personality

Realistic people have structured patterns of thought and tend to live in the present rather than the past or future. They perceive themselves as having mechanical and athletic ability. They tend to be more conventional in attitudes and values because the conventional has been tested and is reliable. They possess a quality of persistence, maturity, and simplicity. Realistic types are found in occupations related to engineering, skilled trades, and agricultural or technical vocations.

### Realistic Environment

The realistic environment is structured, with clear goals and lines of authority. People who work in this environment prefer "hands-on," physical, and/or mechanical jobs, generally outdoors. These workers rely on tools, equipment, or machines. They tend to have casual dress and are focused on tangible results.

### Illustrative Occupations

| | |
|---|---|
| Aircraft Mechanic | Forest and Conservation Worker |
| Agriculture Inspector | Forging Machine Operator |
| Automotive Mechanic | Hazardous Materials Removal Worker |
| Automotive Service Technician | Heating & Air Conditioning Mechanic |
| Baker | Insulation Worker |
| Bindery Worker | Janitor and Cleaner |
| Brickmason and Blockmason | Laundry Worker |
| Bus Driver | Landscaping Worker |
| Bus & Truck Mechanic | Logging Equipment Operator |
| Carpenter | Machinist |
| Ceiling Tile Installer | Meat, Poultry, Fish Cutter |
| Construction Inspector | Mechanical Engineer |
| Cook | Painter |
| Desktop Publisher | Plumber, Pipefitter & Steamfitter |
| Drywall Installer | Pest Control Worker |
| Electrician | Printing Machine Operator |
| Electrical Engineering Technician | Roofer |
| Electrical Power Line Installer | Stock Clerk |
| Emergency Medical Technician | Sheet Metal Worker |
| Farm Worker | Telecommunications Line Installer |
| Firefighter | Truck Driver |
| Furniture Finisher | Welder, Cutter, Solderer & Brazer |

http://online.onetcenter.org/explore/interests/Realistic/

Adapted from:
1. Holland, John L. *Making Vocational Choices: A Theory of Careers*, Englewood Cliffs, New Jersey: Prentice Hall.
2. Montross, Liebowitz & Shinkman, *Real People, Real Jobs*, Palo Alto, California: Davies-Black Publishing.

SOICC – NC Career Resource Network                         SELF-ASSESSMENT    7

# Investigative

PERSON AND ENVIRONMENT DESCRIPTIONS

### Investigative Personality

Investigative people are analytical, abstract, and cope with life and its problems by using their intellect. They perceive themselves as scholarly, intellectually self-confident, and having mathematical and scientific ability. They are likely to possess a high degree of originality as well as verbal and math skills. Investigative types are found in occupations related to science, math, and other technical careers.

### Investigative Environment

The investigative environment is non-structured, research oriented, and/or academic. The primary task is to discover, collect, and analyze data or ideas. The environment is scientific, mathematical, medical, or technical in nature.

### Illustrative Occupations

| | |
|---|---|
| Architect | Industrial Technician |
| Biomedical Engineer | Market Research Analyst |
| Cardiovascular Technologist | Mapping Technician |
| Chemical Engineer | Medical Laboratory Technician |
| Chemist | Medical Laboratory Technologist |
| Civil Engineer | Medical Scientist |
| Computer Programmer | Network Administrator |
| Computer Software Engineer | Nuclear Medicine Technologist |
| Computer Systems Analyst | Oceanographer |
| Computer Systems Administrator | Operations Research Analyst |
| Dentist | Optometrist |
| Database Administrator | Orthodontist |
| Drafter | Pathologist |
| Electrical Engineer | Pharmacist |
| Electrical Technician | Physician Assistant |
| Electronics Engineer | Physician |
| Electronic Technologist | Physicist |
| Environmental Engineer | Psychiatrist |
| Food Technologist | Psychologist |
| Forest Technician | Radiologic Technician |
| Forester | Radiologic Technologist |
| General Practitioner | Speech Language Pathologist |
| Geoscientist | Surgical Technologist |
| Health and Safety Engineer | Veterinarian |

http://online.onetcenter.org/explore/interests/Investigative/

Adapted from:
1. Holland, John L. *Making Vocational Choices: A Theory of Careers*, Englewood Cliffs, New Jersey: Prentice Hall.
2. Montross, Liebowitz & Shinkman, *Real People, Real Jobs*, Palo Alto, California: Davies-Black Publishing.

# Artistic

## PERSON AND ENVIRONMENT DESCRIPTION

### Artistic Personality

Artistic people tend to rely more on feelings and imagination. They perceive themselves as expressive, original, intuitive, non-conforming, introspective, and independent. They have artistic and musical ability (acting, writing, and speaking), and they value aesthetic qualities. The artistic person is more likely to relate by indirect means through their medium. Artistic types are found in occupations related to music, literature, the dramatic arts, and other creative fields.

### Artistic Environment

The artistic environment is non-structured, creative, and flexible, where unconventional and aesthetic values are rewarded. The focus is usually on the creation of products, ideas, or performance. The environment ranges from arts organizations, film/TV, galleries, and theater to publishing and/or advertising organizations.

### Illustrative Occupations

| | |
|---|---|
| Advertising Manager | Interior Designer |
| Actor | Landscape Architect |
| Artist | Merchandise Displayer |
| Animator | Multi Media Artist |
| Choreographer | Music Director |
| Composer | Musician |
| Dancer | News Analyst |
| Designer | Photographer |
| Editor | Reporter |
| Fashion Designer | Singer |
| Film Editor | Video Editor |
| Floral Designer | Window Trimmer |
| Graphic Designer | Writer |

http://online.onetcenter.org/explore/interests/Artistic/

Adapted from:
1. Holland, John L. *Making Vocational Choices: A Theory of Careers*. Englewood Cliffs, New Jersey: Prentice Hall.
2. Montross, Liebowitz & Shinkman, *Real People, Real Jobs*, Palo Alto, California: Davies-Black Publishing.

# Social

PERSON AND ENVIRONMENT DESCRIPTIONS

### Social Personality

People who have high interest in other people and are sensitive to the needs of others characterize the social personality. They perceive themselves as liking to help others, understanding others, and having teaching abilities. Social people value social activities, social problems, and interpersonal relationships. They use their verbal and social skills to change other people's behavior. They are generally cheerful, scholarly, and verbally oriented. Social types are found in occupations related to teaching, community awareness, and helping/service vocations.

### Social Environment

The social environment consists of people who are harmonious and congenial. Their primary task is to work with people-related problems/issues. The focus is on informing, training, developing, curing, or enlightening others as a team effort.

### Illustrative Occupations

| | |
|---|---|
| Adult Literacy Teacher | Medical Assistant |
| Aerobics Instructor | Middle School Teacher |
| Audiologist | Nursing Aide |
| Clergy | Occupational Therapy Assistant |
| Correctional Officer | Orderlie |
| Coach | Physical Therapist |
| Dental Assistant | Police Officer |
| Dental Hygienist | Postal Mail Carrier |
| Dietetic Technician | Recreation Worker |
| Education Director | Registered Nurse |
| Elementary School Teacher | Religious Activities Director |
| Fitness Trainer | Remedial Education Teacher |
| Funeral Attendant | Respiratory Therapist |
| Home Health Aide | Security Guard |
| Jailer | School Counselor |
| Kindergarten Teacher | Secondary School Teacher |
| Legal Assistant | Social Worker |
| Librarian | Special Education Teacher |
| Licensed Practical Nurse | Vocational Counselor |

http://online.onetcenter.org/explore/interests/Social/

Adapted from:
1. Holland, John L. *Making Vocational Choices: A Theory of Careers*, Englewood Cliffs, New Jersey: Prentice Hall.
2. Montross, Liebowitz & Shinkman, *Real People, Real Jobs*, Palo Alto, California: Davies-Black Publishing.

# Enterprising

PERSON AND ENVIRONMENT DESCRIPTIONS

### Enterprising Personality

Enterprising people are adventurous, dominant, and persuasive. They place high value on political and economic matters and are drawn to business and leadership roles. Enterprising people perceive themselves as popular, self-confident, and social, possessing leadership and speaking abilities. Enterprising types are found in occupations pertaining to sales, supervision of others, and political and non-political leadership and managerial positions.

### Enterprising Environment

The enterprising environment is driven by results. The focus is usually on the promotion of services or products. It can be in a large or small organization or entrepreneurial in nature.

### Illustrative Occupations

- Administrative Services Manager
- Advertising Sales Agent
- Amusement Attendant
- Athlete
- Attorney
- Bartender
- Child Care Worker
- Claims Adjuster
- Claims Investigator
- Computer Manager
- Construction Manager
- Cosmetologist
- Cost Estimator
- Counter Clerk
- Criminal Investigator
- Demonstrator
- Detective
- Dispatcher
- Flight Attendant
- Food Service Manager
- Hairdresser
- Lawyer
- Occupational Therapist
- Producer
- Property Manager
- Public Relations Manager
- Real Estate Sales Agent
- Rental Clerk
- Retail Salesperson
- Recreation Attendant
- Securities Agent
- Telemarketer
- Travel Agent
- Waiter or Waitress

http://online.onetcenter.org/explore/interests/Enterprising/

Adapted from:
1. Holland, John L. *Making Vocational Choices: A Theory of Careers*, Englewood Cliffs, New Jersey: Prentice Hall.
2. Montross, Liebowitz & Shinkman, *Real People, Real Jobs*, Palo Alto, California: Davies-Black Publishing.

# Conventional

PERSON AND ENVIRONEMNT DESCRIPTIONS

## Conventional Personality

Conventional people are practical, neat, organized, and work well in structured situations. They feel most comfortable with precise language and situations where accurate accounting is valued. They perceive themselves as conforming, orderly, and having clerical and numerical abilities. They make good subordinates and identify with people who are strong leaders. Conventional types are found in occupations related to accounting, business, computational, secretarial, and clerical occupations.

## Conventional Environment

The conventional environment is structured, business-like, and has clear rules and policies. The focus is on systematic manipulation of data, information, numbers, or monies. People who work in this environment tend to be conservative in nature and focused on bottom-line results.

### Illustrative Occupations

| | |
|---|---|
| Accountant | Information Clerk |
| Administrative Assistant | Interviewer |
| Auditing Clerk | Legal Secretary |
| Auditor | Library Assistant |
| Bank Teller | Library Technician |
| Bill Collector | Maid |
| Bookkeeping Clerk | Medical Record Technician |
| Cashier | Medical Transcriptionist |
| Certified Public Accountant | Medical Secretary |
| Computer Support Specialist | Office Clerk |
| Customer Service Representative | Pharmacy Technician |
| Health Technician | Receptionist |
| Housecleaner | Respiratory Therapy Technician |
| Human Resource Assistant | Teacher Assistant |

http://online.onetcenter.org/explore/interests/Conventional/

Adapted from:
1 Holland, John L. *Making Vocational Choices: A Theory of Careers*, Englewood Cliffs, New Jersey: Prentice Hall.
2. Montross, Liebowitz & Shinkman, *Real People, Real Jobs*, Palo Alto, California: Davies-Black Publishing

SOICC – NC Career Resource Network         SELF-ASSESSMENT   12

# Chapter 21
# Questionnaire

The questions presented below are questions that should be answered. Some may be difficult to answer. If not answered now, time will eventually make you consider these questions.

**FOR HIGH SCHOOL/COLLEGE STUDENTS:  YES   NO**

| | | | |
|---|---|---|---|
| 1. | Do you have plans for a career profession or a job after High School or College? | | |
| 2. | Have you researched your chosen profession? Reviewed the industry trend? | | |
| 3. | Will you have a job **after** High School or College graduation? | | |
| 4. | Have you talked to anyone about this? | | |
| 5. | Will your chosen profession provide a lifestyle for you and/or your family? | | |
| 6. | Do you have a backup plan if your first choice fails or is not immediate? | | |
| 7. | Do you plan to live; (a) By yourself? (b) With relatives? Or (c) With friends? | | |
| 8. | Are they willing to let you live with them for a while? If so, how long? | | |
| 9. | Do you know the financial and emotional cost to live with the choices above? | | |
| 10. | Are there concerns about privacy issues? | | |
| 12. | Will you be paying rent? | | |
| 13. | Will your chosen profession or job afford this choice? If not, then what? | | |
| 14. | With only a High School education, can you make it on your own? | | |
| 15. | Does the future frighten you? | | |
| 16. | Are you afraid to be by yourself? | | |

|  | QUESTIONS FOR YOUNG ADULTS: | YES | NO |
|---|---|---|---|
| 1. | Are you currently employed in a job or career profession? | | |
| 2. | In your mind, does your future look promising? | | |
| 3. | Do you have plans beyond where you are at the present moment? | | |
| 4. | Have you written anything down? | | |
| 5. | If so, are you on track with your present plans? | | |
| 6. | If Not, then what? Have you sought advice concerning this? | | |
| 7. | Does your job or profession support your *desired* standard of living? | | |
| 8. | Are there concerns about credit issues? | | |
| 9. | Are there family issues to consider before moving on? | | |
| 10. | Are there relationship uncertainties? | | |
| 11. | If so, do you have plans to change it? | | |
| 12. | Have you considered your eventual lifestyle? | | |
| 13. | Are you making plans for it? | | |

| | QUESTIONS FOR PARENTS: | YES | NO |
|---|---|---|---|
| 1. | Have you talk to your child about his or her life **outside** of your home? | | |
| 2, | Have you been actively monitoring your child's progress through High School and/or College? | | |
| 3. | Are you willing and ready to let them go? | | |
| 4. | Do you have a time frame in mind? What age? At what moment? | | |
| 5. | Have you adequately **prepared** them to be responsible adults? | | |
| 6. | Have you given them life survival skills? | | |
| 7. | Have you discussed their job opportunities after High School or College? | | |
| 8. | Is their chosen field worth pursuing as a profession or a hobby? | | |
| 9. | Do they have other options? | | |
| 10. | If they leave home and can't find employment, will they come back home? | | |
| 11. | Are you willing and prepared to take care of them as an adult child? | | |
| 12. | If they graduate from college, will they still come back home to live? If so, how long? | | |
| 13. | Have you counted this cost? Have they? | | |
| 14. | Will they be Grown & Gone? **Or** Grown and still at Home? | | |

Chapter 22

# <u>If you can:</u>

Determine where you
want to be
5-10-25 years from now

Determine the lifestyle
you wish to have

Determine the income
and/or events
to support that lifestyle

Determine what you want
to be said about you

**Then begin your life's journey with the end results in mind**

Start Sowing Seeds Now For Your
Desired Results

It is my sincere hope that this book has "provoked you" into thinking about <u>your</u> life and how you intend to:

## **S**tart your journey

## **R**eview your journey

## **C**omplete your journey

## <u>It's All Up To You!</u>

***Notes and Decisions***

Order this book online at:

# www.amazon.com

# E.F.G.T.
## Empowering Future Generations Today